PR
281
•T5
1966
Cop.2

Thomas, Percy
  Goronwy, 1875-.

English literature
  before Chaucer

10.95

DATE			

© THE BAKER & TAYLOR CO.

ENGLISH LITERATURE BEFORE CHAUCER

BY

P. G. THOMAS, M.A.

HASKELL HOUSE
Publishers of Scholarly Books
NEW YORK
1966

published by

HASKELL HOUSE
Publishers of Scholarly Books
30 East 10th Street • New York, N. Y. 10003

PRINTED IN UNITED STATES OF AMERICA

PREFACE

In the following pages an attempt has been made to supply an adequate basis for the study of pre-Chaucerian literature.

The author has spared no effort to keep himself in touch with the results of modern research, but it would be impossible to indicate all the writers—English, American, or German—to whom he has been, from time to time, indebted.

It will, perhaps, suffice to mention, among English scholars, Professors Skeat, Gollancz, Saintsbury, Ker, and Chambers, and, from the other side of the water, Professors Bruce, Klaeber, Lawrence, Schofield, and Wells, the latter of whom has been largely followed in the difficult matter of nomenclature.

Further, a general indebtedness to the writings of Ten Brink, Brandl, Sarrazin and Sieper must be acknowledged, as well as to the *Cambridge History of English Literature*, and the recently published *Histoire de la littérature française* of Bédier and Hazard.

A bibliography of Early English literature is accessible in the *Cambridge History*.

LONDON,
September, 1924.

v

CONTENTS

PART I.—THE ANGLO-SAXON PERIOD

PART II.—THE MIDDLE ENGLISH PERIOD

PART I

THE ANGLO-SAXON PERIOD

I. ORIGINS

An investigation into the sources of English literature
will carry us back into the period before the Norman
Conquest, and, if we pursue the quest far enough, into
that continental period, which ante-dates the settlement
of the Germanic tribes in England. The time has gone
by, in which it was possible to speak of Chaucer as the
"father of English poetry." Even Cynewulf, a discovery of the nineteenth century, is far removed from the
period of origins, while Old English literature, in general,
is a product of an advanced civilisation.

The English belong by blood-relationship to the great
Germanic stock, represented by the Goths, Scandinavians,
and West Germanic peoples. For centuries, this stock
was engaged in a fierce struggle with Rome, which ended
in the downfall of the Empire. We are not left in complete doubt as to the character of the Germanic tribes
during this primitive period,—a *catena* of authorities,
Cæsar, Tacitus, Pliny the elder, Ammianus Marcellinus,
Procopius, and Jordanes, come to our rescue, and provide us, at the same time, with valuable geographical
data.

The most considerable of these authorities, Tacitus,
speaks of Tuisco, Mannus, Nerthus, and Woden as deities
worshipped by the Germans during his day, and specula-
tion has extended the list. He refers to the custom of
farming land, to great feasts, in which the tribes participated, to dwellings constructed partly above, partly
beneath the ground, to decorated halls, to the games that
were indulged in, such as dice-playing and chequers.

It has been suspected that the Roman historian's picture of Germanic civilisation is somewhat highly coloured, but there must be a large measure of truth in his account of the social order, and in the stress he lays on their observance of chastity. The institutions of the folk-moot, of the *wergild*, and of cremation appear, likewise, to date back into primitive times. A noteworthy feature of early Germanic society was the position accorded to women. If deeds were the function of men, wisdom was that of women, and later Germanic literature reflects this division of functions fairly clearly.

In the first and second centuries of the Christian era, the ancestors of the English people, the Angles, Saxons, and Jutes, appear to have been located to the east of the Elbe, though their relative situation has not been exactly determined, there being difficulties with regard to the Jutes. Under pressure from without and as a result, possibly, of internal feuds, they began, at the end of the fourth, or the beginning of the fifth, century, to migrate to Britain, where, for several centuries, they were occupied with the tasks of fusion and settlement.

II. OLD ENGLISH POETIC STYLE

The poetry of the Anglo-Saxon period has several characteristics, which serve to differentiate it from that of later English. From a formal point of view, its metre and diction present peculiarities.

Compared with Romance, Old English poetry was accentual rather than syllabic. Every *verse* (or line) is divided into two parts, known as *hemistichs*, the construction of which has been exactly determined. Of the normal

hemistich there are five main varieties, types A, B, C, D,
E, illustrated by the following examples :

A. Wídĕ wárođaš
B. þŏnŏn Éomǽr wŏc
C. þŏnĕ sĕléstằn
D. Síge-Scŷldìngŭm
E. édwèndĕn cwŏm

Two hemistichs are joined together by *alliteration* to
form a verse, the alliteration being attached to stressed
syllables only. Any vowel may alliterate with any other,
but a consonant only with itself. The laws of consonantal
alliteration vary somewhat at different periods. In
Bēowulf, the combinations sp, st, sc alliterate only with
themselves, while palatal and guttural 3 appear to be
kept apart in late West Saxon poetry. The stressed
syllables are represented, in the first place, by nouns and
adjectives, infinitives and participles, but finite verbs,
adverbs, and even pronouns, prepositions, and conjunc-
tions may fall under the stress. The sub-stress (indicated
by the grave accent) falls upon the second syllable (usually long) of trisyllabic words, or upon monosyllables,
subordinated to a preceding stressed monosyllable, but
not sufficiently weak to fall into the *sinking*, or unstressed
element of the foot. The main stress must fall upon a
long syllable, i.e. a syllable containing a long vowel or
diphthong, or a short vowel or diphthong, followed by
two consonants (two short syllables may be made equiva-
lent to one long by *resolution*). In type C, however, the
second stress may fall upon a short syllable. The closed
character of the syllable is, as a matter of fact, the important matter, not the length of the vowel nor the occurrence
of two succeeding consonants. In the following hemistich,
a sub-variety of B, the second stress falls quite legitimately
upon *wæs* :

þǟ hìm ắlúmpĕn wǽs.

Double alliteration in the first hemistich depends upon
the nature of the stressed syllables : in the second hemi-

stich this does not occur normally. In *Bēowulf*, and particularly in later poems, cross alliteration is sometimes employed ; e.g. :

B. Ic̆ d̄ē frŷmd̄a̋ Gód, aňd frófrĕ Gǽst. B.

Rhyme, as a link between verses, occurs only sporadically, and then, mainly, in suffixes. Leonine rhyme is found as early as *Bēowulf* :

D. Ēod̆ĕ ŷrrĕ-mŏd ; hĭm ŏf ĕagŭm stŏd B.

Traces of stanzaic division, possibly accidental, have been detected in O.E. epic, for example, in the four-line arrangement of *Bēowulf* (ll. 312–19, etc.). The use of the refrain,

That passed over, this likewise may,

in *Dēor's Complaint*, makes it certain that some kind of stanzaic division was adopted in early times by elegiac poets. The so-called *First Riddle*, again, shows clear traces of stanzaic arrangement, and is, probably, to be classed as a dramatic lyric. But there is nothing approaching the drama proper in the pre-Conquest period ; the dominant types are the epic and the lyric.

Every language, in its primitive stages, displays a poetic vocabulary in marked contrast to that of its prose, and this is true, though to a less extent, of the later stages of languages. Old English poetic diction, like Greek or Sanskrit, was rich in synonyms, not always capable of being differentiated from one another. For example, the word " sea " was represented, both in prose and poetry, by *sǣ*, but poetry can draw upon a host of other terms, *brim, wær, hærn, sǣ-strēamas, swanrād, holma begang, here-strǣta, hwæles ēđel, ȳđa gewealc, fisces bæđ, sǣ-beorgas, hwæl-mere, gārsecg, holmweg, ārwela,* etc. Periphrastic expressions, such as *fisces bæđ,* " bath of the fish," known technically as *kennings,* are characteristic of early Germanic poetry, in general. Some of these were directly based on Latinisms, e.g. *drihten wereda* = dominus exercitum, Lord of hosts, and *ælda barn* = filii hominum, sons of men.

Side by side with the native, there was a large Latin element in the Old English vocabulary. Of the latter, prose provides the bulk of the instances, but words like *dēofol*, *scrīfan*, *draca* penetrated into poetry. It is particularly interesting to observe how ideas represented by classical words found expression in native elements, " sacrifice " being rendered by *onsegednes*, " Saviour " by *Hǣlend*, " disciple " by *gingra*, " devil " by *grynsmið*, " angel " by *ǣrend-gāst*, and so on.

A striking characteristic of Old English poetic style was *parallelism*, the repetition of an idea in a variety of expressions. In the following lines from *Cædmon's hymn*, the words and phrases italicised stand for a single idea, that of " God," but the series of metaphors serves to enrich that idea in accordance with poetic requirements :

Nū scylun hergan   *hefænrīcæs ward*
Metudæs mæcti   end his mōdgiðanc,
uerc *uuldurfadur* ;   suē hē uundra gihuæs,
ēci Dryctin,   ōr āstelidæ.

Apart from merely formal characteristics, Old English poetry is characterised by a note of lofty seriousness. " Death is better than a life of reproach," exclaims Wiglaf towards the end of the *Bēowulf* epic, and the same thought finds an echo in *Maldon*. Seriousness and didacticism go hand in hand, and the tendency to instruct finds expression in concise gnomic lines, embedded in epic and lyric alike, e.g. :

A man ought to control his strong spirit and hold it with constancy, and be pure in his relations with wise men (*Seafarer*, ll. 109–10).

The elegy was naturally a favourite form with a race so prone to subjectivity as the Anglo-Saxon, and a sense of regret for days gone by is apparent in most of the shorter poems, like the *Wanderer*, the *Seafarer*, and the *Ruin*. Humour, if we may take it as such, assumes somewhat grotesque forms. Compare the following :

A chief of the Geats severed one of them from its life, from its conflict with the waves, so that the hard war-arrow stuck in its heart : it was the slower in swimming in the wave, since death took it off. (*Bēowulf*, ll. 1432–36.)

III.   ANGLO-SAXON KINGDOMS AND THEIR DIALECTS

The Germanic invaders, who began to come over to Britain about the end of the fourth century, consisted of many tribes, most of whom were absorbed into the greater stocks of Angles, Saxons, and Jutes.   According to the *A.S. Chronicle*, Hengest and Horsa landed in 449 A.D. at Ebbsfleet in Thanet, at that period an island, separated from the mainland by the river Wantsum. In 477, the South Saxons landed near Selsea Bill, giving its future name to the district of Sussex.   The Germanic invaders, as a whole, had taken as their point of attack the old *litus Saxonicum* or Saxon shore, extending from the Wash to Southampton Water.   For a long period, it seemed likely that geographical conditions would prevent their advance into the heart of the country.   Not until the West Saxons and the northernmost section of the Angles discovered vital points was the defence of the Celts to prove hopeless.

The unity of Britain was arrived at only after a prolonged struggle between the separate tribes of invaders. The Jutish settlement of Kent was the first to rise to prominence under Æthelbert.   According to Bede, Æthelbert had established his lordship over the kings south of the Humber, by 597.

He was the third of the English kings that had the

sovereignty of all the southern provinces that are divided from the northern by the river Humber and the borders contiguous to the same. (*Ecclesiastical History*, II, 5.)

Æthelbert's marriage with Bertha, daughter of the Frankish king, Charibert, brought him into contact with the mainland, and, in consequence, with the Christian faith. Kent was christianised in 597, and from Kent missionaries went forth to renew the face of Britain.

The rise of Northumbria is associated with the name of Æthelfrith. To crush the remnants of the rival house of Deira, who had fled into N. Wales, Æthelfrith advanced against the Welsh, and, as a result of a victory at Chester, *c.* 615, succeeded in establishing his supremacy from the Irish to the North Seas. During the reign of Eadwine, Æthelfrith's successor, Northumbria entered into relationship with Kent, and came under the influence of the new faith. Under Penda, the son of Wibba, Mercia rose for a time to the headship. The greatest warrior of his age, Penda was, at the same time, the typical representative of heathendom. He strengthened himself by defeating the West Saxons at Cirencester, after which he turned upon Northumbria. Two Northern kings, Eadwine and Oswald, fell in conflict with Penda, but, in the battle of Winwæd, the Mercian king himself was slain, and his kingdom was reduced to her ancient boundaries.

The peaceful years of Northumbrian history followed upon the fall of Ecgfrith at Nectansmere towards the close of the seventh century, and, for a time, Northumbria became the "literary centre of Western Europe." In the second half of the eighth century, Mercia rose to prominence once more under Offa, her last great king, but, with the beginning of the ninth century, Wessex under Ecgberht acquired the headship, and, henceforward, it was the peculiar task of her rulers to secure the unification of Britain.

The eighth century was the flourishing period of Old English poetry, the development of which is associated with the districts of Northumbria and Mercia. But, after the rise of Wessex to supremacy among the kingdoms, the Northern poems were transcribed into West-Saxon, and have come down to us in that dialect. The North was the true home of poetry during the pre-conquest period, though she was robbed of her inheritance. The specimens of the Northumbrian and Mercian dialects, which have been preserved, are of philological rather than literary interest.

To the very beginning of the eighth century belong the *Epinal,* the *Erfurt,* and the *Leiden glosses,* the earliest specimens of the Mercian dialect. The earliest specimens of Northumbrian are *Cædmon's hymn* and *Bede's death-song,* of the first half of the eighth century. Some of the *Kentish charters* have been assigned to the seventh century. The chief example of ninth-century Mercian is to be found in MS. Vespasian A 1: of ninth-century Kentish in the *Charters.* To the tenth-century belong the *Durham Book* and the interlinear translation of the *Gospels of Mark, Luke and John* (Rushworth[2]), both representative of Northumbrian. A tenth-century specimen of Mercian occurs in the translation of the *Gospel of Matthew* (Rushworth[1]): Kentish of the same period is represented by the *Kentish Hymn* and *Psalm.*

IV. CÆDMON AND HIS SCHOOL

Cædmon is the first of the Old English poets, whose name has come down to us. In Bede's *Historia Ecclesiastica Gentis Anglorum,* Book 4, will be found the oft-quoted account of how the poet came to acquire his art. It would appear that the lives of Cædmon and Bede overlapped, since Bede was born in 673 and Cædmon's death is assigned to 700. It is, therefore, probable that Bede's account of Cædmon may be relied upon. A specimen of the poet's work, in the Northumbrian dialect, is provided in the Moore MS. of Bede's *History*, with the accompanying note, "Primo cantavit Cædmon istud carmen." The text of the hymn is as follows :

Nū scylun hergan	hefænrīcæs uard
Metudæs mæcti	end his mōdgiđanc,
uerc uuldurfadur ;	suē hē uundra gihuæs,
ēci Dryctin,	ōr āstelidæ.
Hē ǣrist scōp	ælda barnum
heben til hrōfe,	hāleg scepen.
Thā middungeard,	monncynnæs uard,
ēci Dryctin,	æfter tīadæ,
fīrum foldu,	Frēa allmectig.

It is probable that this version was written down during the first half of the eighth century, so that we are brought near to Cædmon's period. Nothing else can be assigned with certainty to his authorship. There is, however, a mass of poetry preserved in MS. Junius XI, which it was once customary to regard as Cædmon's work. The MS. owes its name to Junius, who printed the contents in 1655. Modern research has shown that the manuscript consists of two parts,—the first containing the so-called *Genesis*, *Exodus*, and *Daniel*, the second *Christ and Satan*. Junius had no hesitation in assigning the whole of this work to Cædmon, in view of the following statement made by Bede :

Canebat autem de creatione mundi et origine humani generis et tota genesis historia, de egressu Israel ex Ægypto et ingressu in terram repromissionis, de aliis plurimis sacrae scripturae historiis, de incarnatione dominica, passione, resurrectione et ascensione in caelum, de spiritus sancti adventu et apostolorum doctrina. Item de terrore futuri iudicii et horrore poenae gehennalis ac dulcedine regni caelestis multa carmina faciebat ; sed et alia perplura de beneficiis et iudiciis divinis, in quibus cunctis homines ab amore scelerum abstrahere, ad dilectionem vero et solertiam bonae actionis excitare curabat.

The contents of the Junian MS. agree in large measure with this description, but it is impossible, on internal evidence, to assign the whole to one or even two authors. It is quite possible that Cædmon wrote a number of poems similar in style to the Northumbrian hymn, and that these were used by other authors as a basis for such work as has come down to us.

Genesis, the first poem in the MS., consists of two parts, *Genesis A* and *Genesis B*, which have been proved to be of separate authorship. In 1875, Sievers showed that ll. 235–851 (*Genesis B*) differ from the rest of the poem in language, style, and metre, and that this part of the poem is closely related to the Old Saxon *Heliand*. Some twenty years later, a number of Old Saxon verses were discovered in the Vatican library, one of which corresponded with that particular passage in the Old English *Genesis*, which had aroused Sievers' suspicions. The brilliant hypothesis was, thus, converted into a fact, and, though there is difference of opinion as to whether the poems were translated from Old Saxon or were the work of a Saxon, resident in England, it has been impossible ever since to maintain the unity of *Genesis*.

Genesis A (ll. 1–234 and ll. 852 to the close) opens with a eulogy of the Creator, which reminds us of *Cædmon's hymn*. It is, therefore, possible that the author of this section based his poem on material, derived from the poet of Whitby, but now lost. An account of Satan's revolt follows, which theme was afterwards developed by the author of *Genesis B*. The author of *Genesis A* follows the text of scripture fairly closely, though there is some extraneous matter. He is no mere paraphraser, as the descriptions of chaos, of the Flood and of Chedorlaomer's attack on Sodom and Gomorrah prove. But the narrative is not sustained at these levels throughout, and there can be no question as to the intellectual superiority of the author of *Genesis B*.

The conception of Satan and the dramatic force of the presentment constitute the chief merits of *Genesis B*. The sympathetic treatment of Eve is also noteworthy, and, altogether, *Genesis B* is one of the most remarkable products of Old English poetry. There has been much controversy as to whether Milton was acquainted with the Old English *Genesis*, since it appears from a letter written by Isaac Vossius, Junius' nephew, that Milton and his uncle were on friendly terms. The theory is that Junius acquainted Milton with the contents of the Cædmonian MS., parallels like the following being cited in proof :

Is þes ænga stede ungelīc swīde þām ōdrum þē wē ær cūdon (*Gen.* B. 356)

alongside of

O how unlike the place from whence they fell. (*Paradise Lost*, I, 75.)

But it is certain that two poets, writing on the same theme, will have material in common, and it is difficult to realise how Milton, who became blind in 1652, could have made himself minutely acquainted with the contents of an Old English MS., which did not come into Junius' possession until 1651.

The literary qualities of the *Exodus* suggest a third poet. The theme is limited to an episode, and contrasts with the expansive narrative of *Genesis*. The treatment of scripture is very free, with the consequence that an imaginative handling is made possible. The passage dealing with Noah and Abraham (ll. 362–445) has sometimes been regarded as an interpolation, but this view cannot be maintained with certainty.

Daniel is a close rendering of the first five chapters of the *Book of Daniel*, and prosaic in quality. An interesting problem arises in connection with ll. 279–408, which correspond, more or less closely, with the poem in the Exeter Book, known as *Azarias*. This section appears to be of later date than its context, and has been labelled *Daniel B*.

The second part of the Junian MS. contains the poem, which Grein entitled *Christ and Satan*. This section of the MS. is distinct from the first, and, apparently, the work of three new scribes. It is probable that we have to deal with three distinct poems, concerned with (*a*) The Fallen Angels (ll. 1–365), (*b*) The Harrowing of Hell and the Ascension (ll. 366–664), (*c*) The Temptation (ll. 665–733). On metrical grounds, these have been assigned to the second half of the eighth century : they appear to have been written under the influence of Cynewulf.

V. OLD ENGLISH EPIC

Many elements contributed to the making of the popular epic. Starting, as a rule, from an historical foundation, the epic grew by accretion. The heroic poem, which served as its nucleus, expanded under the influence of other heroic poems, until the lines of the original story were transformed, or confused. The full-grown epic, while retaining the heroic character of its original, differed therefrom in its choice of a narrative method, but the problem as to how the border-line between the two was crossed has not been completely solved. The differences between the Old Norse heroic poems, on the one hand, and *Bēowulf*, on the other, may perhaps be taken as illustrating epic-formation at its different stages.

The epic is distinguished by the heroic character of the

deeds and events described. The narrative centres round prominent personages of the past, whose achievements, much idealised and even perverted, are held up for the admiration of a later age. Historical facts may supply the basis of the expanded narrative, but accuracy of fact is no part of the poem's qualification. The heroes of *Germania* had become the common property of the separate tribes, and lived in their imaginations as embodiments of heroic qualities. Limitations of country, or of date, were easily over-stepped, with the result that, in one and the same poem, Ermanaric (fourth century), Attila (fifth century), and Alboin (sixth century) are introduced in juxtaposition, while *Bēowulf* selects its characters, systematically, from abroad.

The heroic character and the heroic exploit necessitated a style in keeping : hence the stately and dignified tone of the epic, which tends, at its best, towards that ideal of simplicity and directness, demanded of the highest forms of poetry. Further, the range of the epic permitted of a large episodic element, whereby it came to differ radically from tragedy. There is, however, a concise type of epic, exemplified by the *Hildebrandslied*, in which episode is dispensed with, and the tragic note forced into prominence.

The oldest examples of Germanic epic are of popular origin, born of the beliefs and traditions of the people. Despite the changes they underwent at the hands of courtly poets, they retain traces of their origin, and continue to make a universal appeal. The epic of a later date, *Paradise Lost*, for example, is further removed from popular sympathies, more sophisticated, more clearly the work of an individual author, but, nevertheless, heroic, ideal, and didactic, like its predecessor.

Bēowulf, Finnsburg, and *Waldere* represent all that remains of Old English popular epic. Of these, *Bēowulf* is much the most considerable, and deserves the first attention. The poem is preserved in a unique MS., Cotton Vitellius A, XV (British Museum). It was known

to Wanley, though his description of the contents suggests inadequate knowledge :

In hoc libro, qui Poeseos Anglo-Saxonicae egregium est
exemplum, descripta videntur bella quae Beowulfus quidam
Danus ex Regis Scyldingorum stirpe ortus, gessit contra
Sueciae regulos.

The Cottonian library was founded by Sir Robert
Bruce Cotton, who died in 1631. It was sold to the
nation by the fourth baronet, Sir John Cotton, in 1700.
While lodged at Ashburnham House, the library was
damaged by a fire, which broke out in 1731. Over 100
volumes are said to have been burnt, or spoiled, and
some 98 rendered defective. The *Bēowulf* MS. suffered
damage, and a number of the edges, being rendered
brittle, ultimately broke off. In 1786, a Danish scholar,
Thorkelin, travelled to England, and made a copy of
the MS., to which he added a Latin translation. He
also arranged for a second copy by another hand. These
transcripts, which often throw light on passages obscured
by the process of time, are preserved at Copenhagen,
and known as *Thorkelin A* and *B*. The date of the MS.
is generally regarded as late tenth century. The hands
of two scribes are distinguishable, the first ending at
scyran (l. 1939). It should be observed that the lines
of the MS. do not correspond with the verse-lines of the
poem, as arranged by modern editors.

Bēowulf consists of two parts, (*a*) Beowulf at Heorot,
(*b*) Beowulf and the dragon. Further, the first part
may be divided into two sections, dealing, respectively,
with Grendel and Grendel's mother. Earlier theoris⁺s,
headed by Müllenhoff, inclined to suspect that these
divisions represented independent heroic lays, fused
later into one whole. Of the existence of such lays
in early Germanic times there can be no doubt, but we
cannot be certain of their number, nor of the particular
achievement of the poet, who gave to the epic its final
form. The influence of the prose *märchen* must also be

reckoned with, since it is clear that *Bēowulf* has links with some form of the widespread stories of the *Bear's Son* and *Strong Hans*. The metre of *Bēowulf* suggests that it was meant to be read, or at least recited. Its general tone suggests an author associated with the court and belonging to the aristocratic circle of glee-men.

A short summary of the poem will prepare the way for a discussion of origins. Hrodgar, king of the Danes, has built for himself a magnificent palace, called Heorot. His peace is disturbed by the nightly visitations of a monster, Grendel, who carries off the Danish warriors, while they sleep. Hrodgar appeals to Hygelac, king of the Geats, who sends his nephew, Beowulf, to the rescue, accompanied by fourteen followers. Beowulf awaits the appearance of Grendel, tears off his arm, and drives him to his abode beneath the lake. Soon afterwards, Grendel's mother renews the feud and carries off Aeschere, one of Hrodgar's counsellors. Beowulf pursues her to the bottom of the lake, slays her, and cuts off the head of the dead Grendel. In the second part, Beowulf has succeeded to the throne of Hygelac and, in his old age, is called upon to defend his country against the ravages of a fire-breathing monster. Assisted by his faithful companion, Wiglaf, he quells the dragon, but yields up his own life, leaving final instructions as to the care of his kingdom to Wiglaf.

The above summary will suffice to bring out the fact that the scenes and characters of the epic are non-English, though the range of the material has by no means been indicated. In common with all epics on an extended scale, *Bēowulf* is provided with a liberal supply of episodes, the personages of which are practically all drawn from non-English sources. Under other names, they figure elsewhere in history and legend, and serve to prove the ubiquity of the Germanic hero. The names Healf-dene, Hrodgar, Halga, and Hrodulf, in the main body of the story, have been equated with Halfdan, Hróarr, Helgi, and Hrólfr Kraki, in Scandinavian history and

E.L.C.   C legend. Hygelac is most plausibly identified with the Ch(l)ochilaicus of Gregory of Tours, and Beowulf himself with the Boðvarr Bjarki of the *Hrólfssaga*. The episodes greatly increase the number of foreign personages, by the addition of heroes like Finn and Hnæf, Sigmund, Ingeld, Eormenric, Ongenþeow and Weland. Of the episodic figures, Offa alone has any claim to be regarded as a national hero, unless we accept the very doubtful identification of Hengest with the Saxon invader.

Anglo-Saxon readiness to base its expression of national life and sentiment upon foreign material is less difficult of comprehension, if we bear in mind the readiness with which nations, like the French, welcomed Arthurian material. The spirit actuating our epic is none the less English because of its foreign scenes and characters ; a common ideal of honour and justice occupied the minds of poets throughout Germania. But there is a difficulty in explaining the sudden appearance of this mass of foreign legend at the beginning of the eighth century, the supposed date of composition of the poem. It has been assumed that the material was inherited from the original home of the Angles, from a period at which Angles and Danes lived in juxtaposition. This theory, the *lay-theory*, scarcely allows sufficiently for the activity of the poet, who handled the materials in the eighth century. *Bēowulf*, in its final form, is clearly the work of a single writer, to whom we owe the orderly presentment of the material, the uniform treatment of the character of the hero, and the peculiar tone of the sentiment. It has been suggested by Sarrazin that the choice of material was dictated by a revival of interest in Danish history, which came to England about this date from Frisia. In any case, the independence of the *Bēowulf* poet is attested by the systematic way, in which he remoulds his materials into harmony with the Christian standpoint. The Biblical element is no mere interpolation ; it forms the very weft and woof of the poem. Klaeber has succeeded in showing that *Genesis A* lay to the hand of the author of *Bēowulf*, and that it was assiduously imitated, in particular instances. A new chronology is, therefore, indispensable, and, if *c.* 700 be accepted as the date of *Genesis A*, *Bēowulf* must be placed somewhat later.

Bēowulf exemplifies the main characteristics of Old English poetry,—its heroic sentiment, its high seriousness, its deep vein of melancholy. "Dēad bið sēllra eorla gehwylcum þonne edwītlīf" might serve as the text of a discourse on heroic loyalty. The apparent triviality of the story is soon forgotten, submerged beneath the lofty sentiment and the heroic outlook. *Bēowulf* has no claim to be regarded as a patriotic poem; it is rather the glorification of a hero, who lives as an embodiment of universal Germanic ideals.

It is to the *Linguarum Veterum Septentrionalium Thesaurus* (1705) of the antiquary Hickes that we owe the text of the *Fight at Finnsburg* : the MS. has disappeared from its original home in the Lambeth Palace Library. *Finnsburg* is a tragic tale, told with rapidity and vigour, and, though it lacks a beginning and an end, there is no reason to believe that it extended much further, in its original form. It conforms to the concise heroic type, represented by the *Hildebrandslied*. The chief characters of the poem make their appearance in the Finn episode in *Bēowulf*, but, despite this parallel, the situation is not entirely clear. It would appear that Hnæf was treacherously attacked by Finn, or his allies, in the hall of Finnsburg, though the issue of the encounter is left untold. From *Bēowulf*, we gather that Hnæf was actually slain by Finn, who was afterwards forced to make terms with his successor, Hengest. The attack on Hnæf was avenged by Gudlaf and Oslaf (apparently the Gudlaf and Ordlaf of *Finnsburg*), who slew Finn in one of his castles. The *Fight at Finnsburg* opens with a vigorous speech on the part of the besieged leader, in which he warns his men that it is the torches of the foe, and no dawning from the East, that they perceive : the moon shines forth, and deeds of woe arise. Then follows a dramatic account of the incidents of the fight, one of which has been interpreted so as to suggest a parallel to the story of *Sohrab and Rustum*,—Gudlaf and his son, Garulf, fight on opposite sides, the son eventually falling in the fight, though at whose hands we are not told.

In 1860, two vellum leaves containing portions of the story of *Waldere* were discovered in the National Library at Copenhagen. The first fragment consists of a speech, apparently by Hildegyð, Waldere's betrothed, in which she reminds that battle-leader of the virtues of his good sword, Mimming, and of his prowess in the past : Waldere, she declares, may well hope to bring to naught the pride of Gudhere. In the second fragment, Gudhere vaunts the quality of his particular blade, once the property of Theodoric and destined for Widia, who assisted his lord against the giants. Waldere replies, challenging Gudhere to begin the onset.

The story is told in full in the *Waltharius* of Ekkehard, a Latin poem in hexameters. Waltharius (Waldere) and Hiltigund (Hildegyð) have fled from Attila into Burgundian territory, where they are attacked by Guntharius in their rocky stronghold, despite Hagano's attempts to dissuade him. After the slaughter of Guntharius' men Hagano can no longer hold back, but, after a fierce encounter between the three survivors, the struggle terminates peacefully. The scale of the Latin poem suggests that the original *Waldere* was long drawn out, a supposition all the more probable in view of the length of the speeches and the didactic note at the close. The situation in the second fragment is, on the other hand, akin to that in the shorter epic of *Finnsburg*,—a fight against odds. The background of Germanic saga is well illustrated in the brief compass of the English text by the allusions to Wayland, Attila, Theodoric, and the Burgundian chieftains, Gunther and Hagen.

VI. CYNEWULF AND HIS SCHOOL

As far back as the year 1840, Grimm and Kemble simultaneously discovered that certain Old English poems, —*Elene, Christ,* and *Juliana,*—contained, embedded in them in runic letters, a personal name, presumably that of the author : the form of the name varied between Cynewulf and Cynwulf. In 1888, Napier discovered the second form in the poem, known as the *Fates of the Apostles,* and thus extended the list of the poet's works. For more than half a century conjecture has been busy with the Cynewulfian problem, hypothetical lives of the poet have been written, and the canon of his works has been vigorously debated.

The runic passages make it clear that Cynewulf was the author of four poems, which have been arranged conjecturally in the following order,—*Juliana, Fates of the Apostles, Christ,* and *Elene.* The original dialect of these poems was Anglian, possibly Northumbrian ; they have come down to us in West Saxon transcripts. The hypothetical lives are based, primarily, on the runic passages, which are of a subjective character. Of these, the most important is that contained in the *Elene,* written most probably at the close of the poet's life :

Ever till then was strife,
A drooping torch harassed by wellings of care,
Though he in the mead-hall treasures received,
Appled gold. Affliction was oppressed,
Necessity's companion, endured sorrow,
The narrowing rune, when the steed before him
Measured the mile-paths, proudly rushed on,
Bedecked with wires. Joy is lessened,
And pleasure in the course of years ; youth is changed,
The pride of former days. My possession was once
The gleam of youth. Now are my days,
In their appointed time, departed forth,
My life-joys have vanished, as water glideth away,

The rushing floods. Wealth is for every man
Transient beneath the sky. (*Elene*, ll. 1257–71.)

With this passage is associated an account of how the
poet, "fettered with sin," was released from bondage by
a vision of the Cross. It would appear then that Cynewulf, in his youth, had been rewarded with treasures in
the mead-hall, though not necessarily as a minstrel,
attached to a lord. As he grew older, he felt the passing
of youth's gleam, and, for a time, abandoned himself to
grief. Salvation came to him in the form of a vision.
Cynewulf does not deny that he had meditated on religious
themes before the appearance of the vision, but he emphasises the fact that the vision was for him in the nature
of a new revelation. He may, therefore, have composed
religious poems before the date of the *Elene*, while the
reference to his old age does not exclude the possibility of
his having continued to write after the date of the *Elene*.
In addition to these facts, deduced from the poems, linguistic investigation favours the view that Cynewulf
belonged to the second half of the eighth century.

Cynewulf's poems belong to the type of religious epic.
They display much of the old heroic manner, but with
the view-point changed. The subjective note is everywhere prominent, and the poet is interested, first and
foremost, in ideas and emotions. Cynewulf possessed
the artistic temperament in a high degree. His diction,
his metre, his elaborate similes suggest the conscious
artist. He was in close touch with the culture of his
day, and displays an intimate familiarity with Latin
lives of the saints, sermons, and hymns. Above all, he
was possessed of a powerful imagination. But Cynewulf's
style betrays much inequality ; he is unable to sustain
himself on the poetic heights. He has little skill in
fusing together the elements of a poem, and is apt to
lose himself, at times, in vagueness and obscurity.

Juliana is based on a Latin life of the saint, akin
to that printed in the *Acta Sanctorum*. Cynewulf fol-

lows his text closely, but, by omitting certain details, he has succeeded in conveying a more favourable impression of his heroine. The speeches tend to be prolix, though there is a rare charm in the father's opening words :

Thou art my daughter, the dearest and the sweetest to my heart, my only daughter on earth, the light of mine eyes, Juliana !

and this despite the fact that the source lay to hand in the Latin original :

Filia mea dulcissima Juliana, lux oculorum meorum.

There are occasional echoes of *Bēowulf*, and epic passages proving Cynewulf's enthusiasm for the heroic style. At the close, the poet introduces himself as one, who has particular need of the saint's intercession :

I have great need
That the saint should grant me help,
When the dearest of all things part from me,
When the two comrades sever their kinship,
Their great heart-love, and my soul from the body
Fares on its journey, I know not whither,
Ignorant of its future home.

Christ, with its three sections,—the Nativity, the Ascension, and the Day of Judgment,—has claims to be regarded as Cynewulf's finest work. It is true that some of the separatists have attempted to limit his authorship to the second section, extending from ll. 440–867. But this view is based almost exclusively on metrical statistics of uncertain value, and Dietrich's opinion as to the unity of the poem is not lightly to be set aside. The general tone of the *Christ* is lyrical, though there are passages of a semi-dramatic character, e.g. the dialogue between Joseph and Mary, and the speeches of the heavenly messengers. There is no lack of show-pieces, such as the descriptions of the Seraphim (ll. 385 ff.), Nature's gifts (ll. 604 ff.); the endowments of men (ll.

664 ff.), and the Judgment Day (ll. 867 ff.). The poet is limited by the nature of his theme, but, in an ingenious allegory, he has contrived to introduce, at l. 850, one of those sea-passages, in which he always excels. The general sources of the *Christ* have been tracked out : Part I is based on the ecclesiastical antiphons, Part II on the 29th homily of Gregory the Great, Part III on the Latin hymn, *De Die Judicii.*

The short poem, known as the *Fates of the Apostles,* has suggested some interesting problems. In 1871, Sweet hazarded the opinion that the *Fates* was merely an epilogue to *Andreas,* its predecessor in the MS. Sweet's view has been upheld by several scholars, and would seem to be confirmed by Napier's discovery of the runic passage at its close. On the other hand, it has been maintained that the runic passage is an independent piece, unconnected with the *Fates,* and that no argument can be based upon its position. This is an extreme view, and the *onus* of proof rests with the objectors. Less easy to dispose of is the fact that a combination of *Andreas* with both the *Fates* and the runic passage involves the existence of two epilogues. Skeat supposed the epilogue containing the runes to be the later, and made the scribe responsible for the inclusion of the older version. It is still possible to maintain the view that *Andreas* is the work of an imitator, well-versed in the style of the *Elene.* Heroic passages abound in both, and a romantic element of a somewhat crude character suggests a connection between the two.

The legend of Helena and the " Finding of the Cross " is recounted in the *Acta Sanctorum* and the *Legenda Aurea.* The particular version used by Cynewulf is not extant, but it is highly probable that he made use of a Latin, rather than a Greek, text. The same appears to be the case with *Andreas,* though the story is ultimately derived from the Greek legend in the *Acta Apostolorum.* While the framework of both *Elene* and *Andreas* is, thus, taken over from the legendary lives, the poet permits himself great freedom of treatment. Significant expressions remind us, at intervals, of his originals, but the descriptive passages find their natural kinship in Old English epic poetry. The terrors of battle and of the sea, as described in these poems, come from a master hand.

Elene and *Andreas* have the appearance of companion poems, but, if common authorship be denied them, we must have recourse to the theory of a Cynewulfian school, in order to explain their resemblances. A number of other poems have also been ascribed to Cynewulf, from time to time, the special characteristics of which are best explained by some such theory.

There can be little doubt that *Gūðlāc*, as we have it, consists of two parts, the work of independent authors. The view-point is different in the two sections, the second passing lightly over the fiends and concentrating on the circumstances attending the saint's death. *Gūðlāc A* (ll. 1–818), after a preliminary passage, dealing with the various conditions of man on earth, refers briefly to the saint's youth, and proceeds to his conversion and retreat to the wilderness, where he is assailed by fiends and subjected to temptation. In the end, Bartholomew intervenes, and the fiends are compelled to bear Gudlac to his retreat, where he remains to the day of his death, at one with God and Nature. There is little movement in the poem, which is concerned, chiefly, with mental states and heart-burnings. In the second section, *Gūðlāc B*, the poet reminds us how death came into the world, as a result of Adam's sin. Holy men, from time to time, have combatted this evil, as instanced by Gudlac, who led a solitary life for fifteen years, harassed by fiends, until, at length, sickness overcame him. In this second poem, a faithful servant ministers to Gudlac's wants, and plies him with questions. *Gūðlāc A* is not distinguished by imaginative writing, though it possesses a certain charm. An interesting psychological passage emphasises the differences between youth and middle-age (ll. 495-504), and there is a pleasing picture of the hermit's retreat,

" where the song of birds is sweet, the earth abloom, and cuckoos herald the year " (ll. 744–45). The author professes to have been a contemporary of the saint, thus ruling out Cynewulf. On the other hand, it is difficult to deny *Gūðlāc B* to the author of the signed poems. The rhymes, both leonine and final, of the opening passage are characteristically Cynewulfian, if not inevitably his. Artistically, *Gūðlāc B* is much in advance of its predecessor, and the first author has nothing so charming as the account of the birds, that flew to the hermit's hand, nor so touching as the picture of the saint in his last sickness. Nor is the splendour of the closing passage, where the beam of light arises from the saint's body, hastening the departure of the messenger on his sea-voyage, paralleled in the earlier poem. Some controversy has arisen as to whether the lines, formerly printed at the end of *Christ* (ll. 1664–92), are not actually the opening of *Gūðlāc*. It seems probable that this is so (cf. ll. 26–29 with ll. 46–50), in spite of the opposed view that they represent an independent poem. Both *Gūðlāc A* and *Gūðlāc B* appear to have been based on a Latin life of the saint by Felix of Croydon, but the source is handled much more freely in the second. The fact that Gudlac was a Mercian (*d.* 714) has led some of those, who ascribe *Gūðlāc B* to Cynewulf, to assign the poet also to the same district.

The tendency to ascribe anonymous poems to known authors has resulted, further, in the ascription of the *Phoenix* to Cynewulf. Thorpe, Ten Brink, and Sweet pronounced the poem his, the opposite view being maintained by Bradley and Sievers. The *Phoenix* and the signed Cynewulfian poems have a certain word-element in common, along with a tendency towards the employment of rhyme :

ne forstes fnǣst	ne fȳres blǣst
ne hægles hryre	ne hrīmes dryre
ne sunnan hǣtu	ne sincaldu

(Phoen. ll. 15–17, cf. Elene, l. 1237 ff.)

But the subject of the *Phoenix* belongs to another category than that of the signed poems, and, though it is, by no means, impossible that Cynewulf should have interested himself in the mediæval version of the theme, the superior workmanship of the poem tells against his claim. The legend, ultimately of Eastern origin, is referred to by Herodotus and by Ovid. In the early Christian era, there appeared a poem, *De Phoenice*, ascribed to Lactantius, from which the *Phoenix* is derived. Verbal resemblances associate the two poems, Latin and Old English. The symbolism of the latter part of the *Phoenix* is, however, derived from patristic literature.

Perhaps the most interesting of the problems of Old English poetic authorship concerns the *Dream of the Rood*, which corresponds, in subject-matter and phrase, with the lines on the Ruthwell Cross. Much significance has been attached to the inscription on the cross, but the rendering " Cædmon made me " is highly doubtful, and the reference, in any case, uncertain. On the other hand, the theme of the *Dream* is related to the closing passage of *Elene*, possibly a mere coincidence due to the new position assigned to the cross, in worship, by Pope Sergius. The language of the Ruthwell Cross is almost certainly pre-Cynewulfian, and, though the *Dream* itself has points of contact with Cynewulf, certain features suggest that it, also, belongs to an earlier period. It is uncertain whether the lines on the cross represent the nucleus of the *Dream*, or merely a series of extracts from that poem, though the latter view is more probable. In any case, the combination of long and short lines in the *Dream* tends to associate it, in part, with the older Cædmonian School. The *Dream of the Rood* must always rank among the finest products of the Old English muse. Its personification is much more than a literary convention ; passion permeates the whole. Its brooding melancholy is deeper than Cynewulf's, and the possibility that the author of *Elene* was himself indebted to native models needs to be borne in mind.

VII. OLD ENGLISH LYRIC

Old English poetry possesses few, if any, examples of pure lyric. A variety which has been distinguished as heroic lyric is, however, well represented by *Wīdsīð* and *Dēor's Complaint*. The term, dramatic lyric, has also been applied to these poems, and the list extended by the addition of the so-called *First Riddle*, the *Seafarer*, the *Wanderer*, the *Wife's Complaint*, and the *Husband's Message*. From another point of view, the *Wanderer* has claims to be regarded as an elegy, along with the *Ruin* and the *Grave*. But lyricism is closely bound up with form. In certain moods, the Anglo-Saxon poet was capable of imparting a strong emotional tone to the epic line, as the poems of Cynewulf testify, but the continuous lyric was rarely attempted. The outstanding examples, *Dēor's Complaint* and the *First Riddle*, followed later by the *Runic* and *Rhyming poems*, survive to show how far the Anglo-Saxons attained to mastery of this type.

Wīdsīð, the " far travelled," is preserved in the Exeter Book, along with *Dēor's Complaint*. The poem consists of two parts, (*a*) a general catalogue of kings, (*b*) a list of persons and tribes visited by the poet. The prologue supplies the names of the poet and of his tribe, the Myrgings ; the epilogue celebrates the bountiful patrons of the glee-man. The names in *Wīdsīð* have given rise to many problems ; they cover a period of, at least, three centuries, even if we exclude the non-Germanic peoples. It is impossible, therefore, to regard the poem as biographical ; it is rather a repertory of historical and geographical material, such as a *scop* would find useful for his poetic business. The interest lies in the more elaborate of the allusions to epic heroes,—Eormanric, Offa, Hroðwulf and Hroðgar, Guðhere, Ælfwine, Eadgils, Wudga and Hama. The personal note becomes prominent in the account of the poet's relations with the lady, Ealhhild, and of his rivalry in song with Scilling.

Like *Widsīð*, *Dēor's Complaint* treats of a minstrel, though in a less cheerful way. In the former, there is no hint of serious rivalry between the poet and Scilling, but Deor has lost his lord's favour, supplanted by a rival, Heorrenda. From the formal point of view, the remarkable thing about *Dēor's Complaint* is the recurrent refrain,

That passed over : this likewise may.

The poet seeks comfort for himself in the woes of others, —Weland, the smith, Beadohild, the ill-starred daughter of Niðhad, the more or less obscure Hild, the Gothic Theodoric, and Eormanric. The stanzas, in which these personages are introduced, vary in length from two to six lines, but end invariably with the refrain. The personal passage, at the close, is expanded to fourteen lines, a portion of which may possibly have been interpolated. For the most part, the allusions are clear, but the identity of Hild has not been satisfactorily made out. The assumption that she is identical with Beadohild involves a double allusion, and a difficulty in the interpretation of the name, Geat. Possibly, Hild stands for Swanhild, in which case the Geat is Eormanric.

With regard to the interpretation of the so-called *First Riddle*, in the Exeter Book, many views have been held. As the title suggests, it has been regarded as a riddle, pure and simple ; on the other hand, the tendency of recent opinion has been to class it as a dramatic lyric, in which case some such title as *Ēadwacer* would be appropriate. But the theory that the personages of the poem are the Norse Sigmund and his sister, Signy, has suggested a rival title, *Signy's Lament*. The vagueness of the back-ground makes it difficult, however, to determine whether the story is to be associated with Odoacer, or with Sigmund. All that can be said with certainty is that we have before us an intensely passionate little lyric, seeking expression in an approximation to the stanzaic form, and making effective use of the refrain :

> Wolf, my Wolf, my longings for thee
> 'Twas they made me sick, thy seldom-comings,
> My sorrowful mind, not lack of food.

The *Wanderer* and the *Seafarer* are companion poems, with material in common. Both display enthusiasm for the wilder aspects of Nature, tinged with a brooding melancholy and a sense of the vanity of earthly things. Within the brief compass of each, the style changes rapidly from the descriptive to the gnomic, from the rhetorical question to the slow-moving expanded passage. How far interpolation need be assumed in explanation of these transitions is a moot point : a blending of paganism with the new faith is characteristic of the later expressions of Anglo-Saxon poetic genius. The close parallel between the closing sections of the poems may, however, point to a common interpolator. The nucleus of both has been assigned to the eighth century ; they are certainly later than the national epic, from which they differ peculiarly in tone. The central note of the *Wanderer* is the longing of an exile for a lost patron, expressed with deep pathos, and emphasised by the contrast between his present situation and the cheerful scenes of the mead-hall. The wanderer himself appears to be a type rather than an actuality, and attempts to associate him with epic cycles are not convincing. The *Seafarer*, with its contrasted pictures of land and sea, has prompted other theories. It has been claimed as a dialogue by Rieger, Kluge, and Hönncher, though none of these critics are agreed as to the division of the speeches. A more plausible view is that of Sweet, who regarded the poem as a monologue, in which an old sailor contrasts the hardships of a seafaring life with its inevitable allurement, and proceeds to illustrate his point by instancing the constant claim upon man of the spiritual life. Both the *Wanderer* and the *Seafarer* excel in vivid sketches of the sea and of sea-birds. This nature-painting represents an important phase in the development of English poetry, while the grave reflective tone links the poems with certain aspects of eighteenth-century literature.

A connection between the *Wife's Complaint* and the *Husband's Message* has been assumed, with some plausibility, by several critics. Unfortunately, the meaning of the former is often obscure. It would appear (if the evidence of the second poem is relevant) that the lady's husband has deserted her, in consequence of a feud. In his absence, she is imprisoned, or has taken sanctuary, in a cave, under an oak, where she bemoans her fate, so unlike that of the majority of lovers. She is confident that her husband's grief is as great as her own, and poignantly expresses her emotion in the concluding outburst,

Woe to her who, with anxious longing, must needs abide her loved one's coming !

Difficulties have arisen owing to the assumption that ll. 17 ff. represent a curse against the husband, but, as Lawrence has shown, the passage may be interpreted quite otherwise. The theory that the poem is an offshoot from the Offa-cycle, and that the ill-treatment of the lady is due to a forged letter, ostensibly from her husband, is ingenious, though it robs the poem of any possible connection with its companion. A connection with the Crescentia legend has been assumed by Stefanovič. The interpretation of the *Husband's Message* presents fewer difficulties, in spite of defects in the text. A lady receives a message from her husband in the form of a rune, which, curiously enough, assumes the part of speaker. He has been separated from her for a time, but bids her join him as soon as she shall hear " the mournful cuckoo sing forth in the grove." He has wealth to set at her disposal, and joyfully renews his old-time vows. In the Exeter MS., the poem follows immediately upon the " Reed " riddle (No. 61), and a pretty guess that the riddle is actually an introduction to the lyric has been hazarded by Blackburn. On the whole, it seems safer to assume that the lyric has strayed into the riddle collection, owing to resemblances between its opening lines and No. 61. It is an attractive theory that the *Husband's Message* supplies the true sequel to the *Wife's Complaint*.

The *Runic* and *Rhyming* poems display a formal connection as experiments in unusual modes. The former consists of twenty-nine stanzas, varying in length from two to five lines : the latter, as its title suggests, is an experiment in rhyme. In the Cynewulfian poems and elsewhere, rhyme makes sporadic appearances, but the elaborate venture, represented by the second poem, is without parallel in Old English literature. The rhyme forms a link, not merely between ends of verses and half-verses, but, as a specific literary ornament, between successive words :

scrīþendscrād glād   þurh gescād in brād :
wæs on lagustrēame lād,   þær mē leoþu ne biglād
                             (ll. 13–14).

This experiment would seem to find its natural place at the close of the Anglo-Saxon poetic period, but it is asserted that the original dialect was Anglian, and that its date may be as early as the eighth century. As regards subject-matter, the *Rhyming poem* has links with the *Ruin*, which describes with much vividness a poet's impressions of a decaying city. The hot baths, introduced at l. 39, have suggested identification with the Roman city of Bath. The reference to the vanished joys of the hall associates the *Ruin* with the first portion of the *Rhyming poem* (ll. 1–42), and with parts of the *Wanderer*.

The short poem, entitled the *Grave* (twelfth century), is the last echo of Old English lyric : a transition poem in regard to both metre and language, it brings the period to a close on a note of gloom.

VIII. DIDACTIC POEMS

It will be convenient to class under the head of didactic verse a number of poems of various ages, all of which exhibit a tendency to instruct, in greater or less degree. Of these, the *Riddles* might well be claimed for other groupings, but their original connection with proverbial literature justifies their inclusion here.

The Old English *Gnomic verses* represent a particular aspect of the wisdom literature of our ancestors. Sententious sayings of a proverbial or moral character, they find expression in detached lines, or series of lines, constructed on the alliterative principle. Ordinarily, the compass of the gnome is brief, but in narrative poetry it is expanded, for purposes of illustration, into the gnomic passage. Contrast the following maxim from the Cottonian Collection :

geongne æþeling   sceolan gōde gesīdas
byldan tō beaduwe   and tō bēahgife

with the expanded passage in *Bēowulf*, ll. 20–25. The gnomic verse represents popular wisdom on the subject of nature, man, and the gods. The point of view is often definitely heathen, sometimes equally definitely Christian. But parallels in other literatures suggest that the nucleus of the collection was pre-Christian,— apart from which theory it would be difficult to explain the reference to Woden, among other things. The style of the verses is bald, with the exception of certain passages of an evidently later date. Of these, the lines on the Frisian wife stand in the very forefront :

Dear is he and welcome
To the Frisian wife,
When the boat comes to land :
His keel is come,
Her husband home,

Her own food-giver :
She invites him in,
Washes his raiment,
Gives him new weeds.
There waits him on shore
What his love needs.

A mixture of old and new may, likewise, be found in
the *Charms*, though the outlook is more definitely pagan
than elsewhere. These charms represent a particular
aspect of Indo-European folk-lore and possess formal
characteristics, paralleled East and West. The opening
passages are frequently epic in character, and this
throughout the range of Indo-European literature. An
invocation follows, addressed to some mysterious power,
and accompanied by the recitation of the magic formula.
For the ridding of the disease, flattery, threats, or even
sympathetic representation is relied upon. Many of
the charms contain detailed directions as to method of
procedure. The incongruity of the material is illustrated
in the juxtaposition of the " mother of earth " and the
Almighty. Charms were recited to promote the fruit-
fulness of earth, to prevent loss of cattle, or to expel
diseases from men and animals. Such literary interest,
as they have, depends entirely upon the epic introduc-
tions.

As examples of literary composition, the *Riddles* are
infinitely superior to anything in this department of
didactic literature : they have a place here, exclusively,
on the ground of their origin in folk-wisdom. The distinction between literary and popular types is always
difficult to maintain. Popular material, in the hands
of an artist, may take to itself literary form, and, con-
versely, a cultured type may degenerate in the mouths
of the people. The comparative method has proved
the world-wide distribution of many riddle-subjects,—
for example, the ice, the ship, the rake. Where a Latin
source can be adduced, the riddle may, certainly, be
classed as literary, though its ultimate origin be popular.

The only distinction, which can be maintained with profit, is that between the highly-finished poetic riddle and its more or less naïve congener. Collections of Latin riddles date back to the century of three-lined hexameter poems, bearing the name of Symphosius (fourth to sixth century). To the seventh and eighth centuries belong the collections of Aldhelm, Tatwine, Eusebius, Boniface, and Alcuin. But, apart from the riddles on the " byrny " and the creation (derived from Aldhelm) and that on the bookworm (based on Symphosius), the Exeter Collection is not greatly indebted to any known predecessors. The solution of the Old English riddles presents many difficulties, as may be judged from the variety of those offered. *Riddle XI*, for example, has been variously interpreted as an anchor (Trautmann), the wake of a ship (Dietrich), a barnacle-goose (Stopford Brooke), a water-lily (Holthausen). The solutions are not, however, equally plausible, and it is likely that the field of agreement will gradually widen. From the literary standpoint, the riddles vary greatly in value, but the best rank among the finest products of Old English poetry.

The poems known as the *Endowments of Men* and the *Fates of Men*, correspond to one another, in part. Between them, they cover the range of man's accomplishments as known to Anglo-Saxon society, but their methods differ. The outlook of the *Endowments* is broader, more discursive : a smaller canvas serves the author of the *Fates*, while his sketches are more elaborate : for example, those of the harp-player and the falconer. The superior art of this latter author is further evinced in the opening section, which is without parallel in the *Endowments*. The various perils, that confront a man in his journey through life, are reviewed, in succession, these being, for the most part, such forms of violent death as were particularly familiar to primitive societies. The pathos of the poem turns upon the prominence accorded to the man's mother,—a witness, in one instance, of her son's doom.

The *Physiologus* is ultimately of Eastern origin : its influence in the West was directly due to Greek and Latin versions. The Old English poem is a mere torso, compared with the Latin (Bern 233 and Royal 2 C XII, Brit. Mus.), but it has not been proved that its original scale was much expanded. Though the Bern version contains thirty-two types of birds and animals, the Old English has three only,—the Panther, the Whale (or shield turtle, according to Cook), and a more or less obscure bird. By a process of symbolism, the panther is taken as a type of Christ and the whale of the devil, the sketch of the latter being, as it happens, the more entertaining. The whale is a source of danger to seamen, its skin resembles a rough stone, and, as it swims near the sand-hills, it is readily mistaken for an island. Sailors rope their ships to this land, which is no land, kindle a fire thereon, and rest themselves, enjoying the weather. Suddenly, they are borne away to the bottom, men and vessel together. The moral in the Latin version runs :

Sic patiuntur omnes qui increduli sunt, et quicumque ignorant diaboli astutias ; spem suam ponentes in eum et operibus eius se obligantes, simul cum illo merguntur in gehennam ignis ardentis.

The tenth-century *Salomon and Saturn* belongs to a widely distributed type, best represented in the Germanic field by the Old Norse *Vafþrúþnismál*. The subject-matter is akin to that of the gnomic verses and of the riddles, though the form is that of the dialogue. Solomon's antagonist is Protean in shape, varying in the different versions between Saturn, Marcolf, Asmodeus, Abdimus, and Hiram, and, despite his reputation as a repository of wisdom, Solomon is sometimes worsted. The contest is essentially one of wits, in which Solomon plays a grave part, as the champion of religion. The tone of his opponent varies according to time and place, with the result that the dialogues sometimes fell into disrepute. In Old English, there were three distinct versions connected with *Salomon and Saturn*, two in metre and one in prose. The verse dialogues differ greatly in tone, the first centering round a vigorous defence of the Pater Noster and concluding with a series of prose passages, bearing an unmistakable relationship to Eastern romance. Yet this version possesses none of the imaginative qualities of the second, and it is in this latter that the kinship between the various types of didactic literature is most clearly exemplified. The lines :

Niht bid wedera þēostrost	nȳd bid wyrda heardost
sorh bid swǣrost byrthen	slǣp bid dēade gelīcost.
	(Kemble's edition, ll. 621–24.)

are purely gnomic : a fully developed riddle on the theme of old age is the subject of ll. 563–82, with a conciser type following in ll. 663–64 : lastly, quitting didacticism, we draw perilously near to the charmed land of romance in Saturn's response to the question concerning " the land where no man may venture."

The metres in the British Museum MS. of *Boethius* (Otho A. 6) extend the scope of didactic poetry over the field of history and philosophy. The poems themselves attribute the authorship to Ælfred. On the whole, they may be regarded as versified renderings of a prose original, with wholesale modifications of the older rules, but without the tendency to sink into mere doggerel. The nature passages attest the poet's skill, and considerable imagination is evinced in the oft-cited lines on Weland, part of a passage in the strain of the familiar mediæval lament :

Hwǣr sint nū þæs wīsan	Wēlandes bān,
þæs goldsmides,	þe wæs gēo mǣrost ?

Another product of the school, the *Menologium* or poetical calendar, is extant in the Abingdon version of the *Chronicle*. The list of saint's-days and the obsolete names of the months impart a curious antiquarian interest to this calendar, while the descriptions of the seasons, particularly of summer, rescue it from mediocrity.

The remaining didactic poems fall together as examples of religious instruction. The oldest, the *Father's Instruction*, a grave discourse on the lines of the *Wisdom of Solomon* and analogous to the Middle English collections, is associated with the names of Ælfred and Hending. The *Address of the Soul to the Body* is extant in two texts in the Exeter and Vercelli MSS. Of the former, the theme is the address of a sinful soul to the body, which it revisits : the Vercelli text, running parallel with the Exeter as far as l. 129, passes, however, at that point to a sequel, in which a virtuous soul displaces the sinful. Though the weakest part of the poem, this has interest as a unique treatment. The material common to the MSS. represents a well-worn theme, handled with much power : the soul reviles the body for its luxuriousness, and expatiates upon its doom in the grave :

Bið þæt heafod tohliden,   handa tolidode,
geaglas toginene,   goman toslitene,
sina beoð asocene,   swyra becowen,
fingras tohrorene,
rib reafiað   reðe wyrmas,
beoð seo tunge totogen   on tyn healfa
hungregum to hroþre.

A poem on the *Last Judgment*, a set of *Prayers*, a *Hymn*, and a *Creed* complete the tale of Old English didactic verse.

IX. HISTORICAL POEMS

The historical poems so called include all that are known to have been inspired by some definite event. It is probable that the older epic contained a nucleus of fact, but this had tended to become submerged under an accretion of legend. In the later historical poetry the events described are practically contemporaneous with the poems, and these have come down to us, as far as can be surmised, in the condition in which they were first produced. The historical poetry of the tenth and eleventh centuries illustrates, in a remarkable way, the strength of the literary tradition. *Judith* and *Maldon* rank amongst the best products of the Old English poetic spirit, and, even where the verse betrays degeneration, the characteristics of the older school are largely present. Alliteration and *kennings* continue in vogue, though with inevitable modifications. The fact, however, that the eleventh century poem, the *Death of Edward the Confessor*, has phrases in common with older epic schools affords a remarkable proof of literary continuity. The inclusion of *Judith* under this category cannot be altogether justified. It is essentially a heroic poem, celebrating the character of a Jewish maiden and her exploits against the Assyrians. The source lies to hand in the apocryphal book so named. It is possible, however, that the poet intended an allegory, and that he was inspired by the heroism of Ædelflæd in her conflict with the Danes. Foster's theory is reinforced by the fact, pointed out by Cook, that Ædelflæd's grandmother bore the name of Judith. The art of literary portraiture is finely illustrated in the contrasted pictures of Judith and Holofernes. Moreover, the poem displays both life and movement, the original being frequently amplified, particularly where the tradition of the heroic school suggested a freer handling. From the metrical point of view, there is additional evidence of elaboration. Lines tend to fall into sequences, distinguished by the employment of identical verse-types (cf. ll. 182–85), or by an alliterative device, whereby the last stressed syllable in a line dictates the alliteration of its successor. Sequences of expanded lines occur frequently, and serve to enhance the dignity of the poem. In Sweet's words, *Judith* shows a combination of "the highest dramatic and constructive power with the utmost brilliance of language and metre."

The *Battle of Maldon* was probably composed soon after 991, the year of Byrhtnod's struggle with Olaf. The vividness of the descriptions suggests the work of an eye-witness, as well as the fact that the name of the Danish leader is omitted. Unfortunately, the poem is incomplete, and we have no means of determining its original compass. The spirit of *Maldon* approaches near to the Homeric. The catalogue of heroes, with their lineages and separate conflicts, is essentially epic while the note of loyalty, permeating the whole, is characteristic not only of Germanic, but of heroic, poetry, in general.

Chronologically, the *Battle of Brunanburh* has precedence over *Maldon*, but its literary importance is considerably less. Its theme is the heroic fight (A.D. 937) in which Ædelstan and Edmund overcame Olaf and his ally, the Scottish Constantine. Both English and Celtic sources bear witness to the grim character of the struggle. Though the compass of the poem is brief, the poet finds opportunity to introduce a spirited reference to the raven, the eagle, and the wolf, the traditional concomitants of battle :

> " Many a carcass they left to be carrion,
> Many a livid one, many a sallow-skin,—
> Left for the white-tail'd eagle to tear it, and
> Left for the horny-nibb'd raven to rend it, and
> Gave to the garbaging war-hawk to gorge it, and
> That gray beast, the wolf of the weald."
>   (Tennyson's trans.)

As we proceed through the tenth and the eleventh centuries, the literary value of these poems steadily declines. The *Recovery of the five boroughs* is merely an ingenious collection of names, with the *Edgar* poems little in advance of it. The remarkable thing is the strength of the literary tradition and its application to novel subjects, like the appearance of the comet in *Edgar's death*. The old metrical rules are still followed, and the *kennings* find parallels in the older poetry. The poem, entitled the *Death of Prince Alfred*, introduces the eleventh century, and presents a curious problem. Thorpe took it for prose, but the sporadic occurrence of rhyme and metrical feet makes it probable that its original form has been modified:

Ne wearð drēorlīcre dæd   gedōn on þison earde
syþþan Dene cōmon   and hēr frið nāmon (ll. 11–12).

A similar problem arises out of the lines on *William the Conqueror*, where rhyme is employed throughout, and the rhythm suggests a popular four-beat metre. *Edward's Death*, however, is not to be associated with the popular school. Despite its date, the second half of the eleventh century, its style surpasses that of the *Edgar* poems, while its observation of the rules is practically faultless.

X. OLD ENGLISH PROSE

In the evolution of literature, prose makes, as a rule, a tardier appearance than verse. The account of Old English prose, has, accordingly, been reserved till this point. As a matter of fact, the oldest examples of Old

English prose appear as early, if not earlier, than any of
the extant verse-pieces. But allowance must be made
for the disappearance of much verse, the existence of
which is involved in our theories of epic origin. Literary
prose is, in any case, a later phenomenon than verse.

The oldest specimens of prose fall under the head of
charters, laws, chronicles, and religious documents. Of
these, the *Charters* comprise such material as grants of
land, leases, and wills. The predominance of Latin, as
a legal language, resulted in its almost exclusive employment in the early charters, and it continued to be used,
side by side with the vernacular, down to the end of the
Anglo-Saxon period. The earliest specimens of native
charters, Saxon or Kentish, reveal no traces of literary
composition, and possess linguistic interest, merely. Not
until the middle of the ninth century, do native charters
begin to be numerous : they have proved invaluable
for the light they throw upon Anglo-Saxon law and
custom.

The oldest English *Laws*, compiled at the beginning of
the seventh century, bear the name of Æthelbert of
Kent. They have survived, however, only in West
Saxon, and possess no linguistic features, which can be
dated earlier than the eighth century. The code opens
upon an ecclesiastical note, by providing against injuries
done to the Church. Then follow tariffs for injuries
done to the king, the *eorl*, and the *ceorl*. The sanctity of
private dwellings is upheld,

Gif man rihthamscyld þurhstind, mid weorde forgelde,

and personal injuries are variously assessed, 30*s.* for
shoulder-laming, 3*s.* for ear-splitting, etc. The teeth
and fingers are separately priced, the latter being distinguished as *þūma, scytefinger, middelfinger, goldfinger,*
and *se lȳtla finger.* The occasional employment of
alliteration suggests an effort towards a more ornate
style. The code of Hlōdære and Ēadric (673–685)
betrays an advance in sentence-structure :

Gif mannes esne eorlcundne mannan ofslæhð, þane ðe sio þreom hundum scll' gylde, se agend þone banan agefe and do þær þrio manwyrð to,

while the *Wihtræd Code* (695) makes some use of endrhyme. As for the *Laws of Ine*, extant only as an appendix to Ælfred's, these date back to the seventh century. After Ælfred's day, codes continued to be produced down to the Conquest, with the result that Old English possesses a series of legal documents more considerable than that of any other Germanic nation.

The *A. S. Chronicle* is, of all the prose products inaugurated during the pre-Ælfredian period, by far the most interesting and important. In its extant form, as represented by its seven MSS., the work is composite, revealing the inter-action of chronicle upon chronicle. It has been the task of modern scholarship to disentangle the threads, and recover its history, from the beginning. No doubt, the *Chronicle* originated in an attempt to distinguish the years, as they passed, by a series of outstanding events. Already at Canterbury, records of the appointment of bishops, of conflagrations, and other events had been set down, in the seventh century. The first organisation of the *Chronicle* is usually assigned to Winchester : it had reached considerable maturity by the time of Æthelwulf (839–858), with whose name the first redaction appears to terminate. In the early part, a good deal of foreign material was afterwards incorporated, the source of which has been sought in some such treatise as the *Recapitulatio*. The famous episode of *Cynewulf and Cyneheard*, selected by Milton as a possible theme for an epic, illustrates the native vigour of the early *Chronicle*, at its best. According to Plummer, separate chronicles existed at different centres, at Winchester, Abingdon, Worcester or Evesham, Peterborough, and Canterbury, between all of which there was more or less interaction. Under Ælfred, the *Winchester chronicle* (Parker MS.) was reorganized and elaborated, the events of 871–897 being handled with much distinction. The interest of the narrative is maintained during the earlier years of the tenth century, and again, towards the close of that century, when the record suddenly terminates. It is noteworthy that records in verse begin to make an appearance from the year 938. About 1001, the *Winchester chronicle* appears to have been transferred to Canterbury. The local notices in MSS. Cott. Tib. A 6 and Cott. Tib. B 1 further suggest the existence of an *Abingdon chronicle*, the shorter version, in the first MS., coming down to 977, the second to 1066. With these, the *Mercian register* (902–925), with its enthusiastic account of Æthelflæd's exploits against the Danes, has been incorporated. Again, the *Evesham chronicle* so-called (Cott. Tib. B. IV) is closely related to that of Peterborough (Laud. Misc. 636), both embodying the Northern annals of 733–806 : this record is further linked to that of Abingdon. The *Peterborough chronicle* introduces much local detail into the early pages of its copy, and, in its closing sections, betrays a Southern interest, for which a Kentish source has been assumed. It contains highly important material for the eleventh century, and concludes with the famous passage concerning the anarchy of Stephen's reign. The deterioration in the general style of the *Chronicle* becomes apparent after a comparison of the records in the Ælfredian sections with those at the close of the Peterborough record.

It was in the second half of the ninth century under Ælfred, that English prose first attained to importance. The activities of the king in the various fields of government, of legal and military organization, have often been emphasised : his interest in literature is attested by the zeal, with which he prepared versions of standard books, adapted alike for cleric and layman. During his reign, the centre of culture was transferred from Northumbria to Wessex, and, though the South was more naturally the home of prose, Wessex was familiarised with the poetical products of the North, in various adaptations. In these respects, the activities of Ælfred's reign invite comparison with those of Charlemagne.

In his endeavour to translate those monuments of Latin scholarship, which seemed best adapted for his educational purposes, Ælfred was assisted by a band of scholars, the Welshman, Asser, Grimbald of Flanders and John of Corvey. The order of his works, though known approximately, has not been exactly determined.

The *Encheiridion* or *Handbook*, was Ælfred's first tentative effort in the direction of literary composition. The book is non-extant, but the term *flosculi*, under which it is referred to by Asser, suggests that it consisted of cullings from various sources. The rendering of these passages into the vernacular inaugurated the king's career as a translator.

The *Hierdebōc* or *Pastoral Care*, a version of the *Cura Pastoralis* of Gregory the Great, is generally placed at the head of Ælfred's translations. Its closeness to the original suggests journeyman-work, but the *Preface* is an excellent piece of original writing, and its function is clearly that of an introduction to the whole series of translated books. The account of the state of learning in Ælfred's day and of the methods employed in his work as translator impart unique interest to this particular section. The book, as a whole, is marred by an excess of allegory, the responsibility for which rests with Gregory.

In the *Historia adversus paganos* of Paulus Orosius Ælfred discovered a work better adapted to the use of the laity than the *Pastoral Care*. To an unsophisticated audience of the ninth century its appeal must have been exclusively historical or geographical, and the thesis, which Orosius set out to expound, would easily be relegated to the background. Recognising its real interest, Ælfred inserted original accounts of the voyages of Ohthere and Wulfstan, which afterwards earned a place for themselves in Hakluyt's great compilation. As a whole, the book is freely manipulated, Ælfred's function

throughout being that of a guide, at liberty to add, or
omit, as he thinks fit. The mass of classical lore, now
introduced to an English audience for the first time,
must have been greatly influential in widening the mental
horizon of its ninth-century readers.

The translation of Bede's *Historia Ecclesiastica* differs
from its predecessors by reason of its close rendering.
Much doubt has arisen as to the authorship, on the ground
both of idiom, and of the exactness with which Mercian
place-names are rendered. The omission of Gregory's
religious activity in England and other matters is still
unexplained. The account of Cædmon, illustrated by
a West Saxon rendering of his famous hymn, constitutes
a section of first-rate interest. Ælfric is the chief authority for Ælfred's authorship.

The composite code of *Laws*, embraced under the name
of Ælfred, betrays both an ecclesiastical and a secular
origin. There are insertions from the Mosaic code, and
a reference to the history of synods throughout the world.
On the other hand, recognition is accorded to Ælfred's
predecessors in Britain by the inclusion of the laws of
Ine, of Offa, and of Æðelbert, which appear, side by side
with Ælfred's ordinances, in a more or less revised form.

The *De Consolatione Philosophiæ* of Boethius was
probably translated towards the close of Ælfred's literary
career, though an earlier date has been assumed, on the
ground that the king derived assistance from Asser. The
abstract character of the book, with its discussions upon
Fate and Providence, would seem, however, to argue
a more mature stage in Ælfred's literary development.
Ælfred displays a certain kinship with the Neo-Platonic
philosopher, and indulges in fervent reflections, in keeping
with his original. The interest of the translation is
greatly enhanced by these additions, while the similes
constitute a highly novel feature.

In the last instance, Ælfred set himself to provide a
rendering of Augustine's *Soliloquia*, the style of which
suggests a connection with the *Consolation*. Once more,

the subject is philosophical, concerned with the nature of God and of the soul. In Book III, new sources are drawn upon. Taken together, the *Soliloquies* and the *Consolation* serve to reveal the depth of Ælfred's religious convictions. The *Preface* to this closing book is in the nature of an Epilogue to the whole series of translated work.

An attempt to estimate Ælfred's position in the history of prose must, necessarily, emphasise the pioneer character of his work. Throughout, we find him in a position of pupilage to Latin models, with the result that a large importation of foreign idioms was inevitable. He has the credit, however, of having recognized the importance of the vernacular, which he established on a sound footing, and, thus, prepared the way for Ælfric and his successors. The importance of his independent insertions, leavened as, they are by his personal enthusiasm, cannot be over emphasised. "He found learning dead, and he restored it ; education neglected and he revived it."

The condition of English monasticism, during the first half of the tenth century, appears to have been deplorable. Ælfred's efforts in the direction of reform had failed to permeate the community, at large, and, for fifty years, the Emperor kings were too much occupied with the Northmen to attend to such matters. Among the clergy, Ælfred found no imitators, save Werferth of Worcester, who translated Gregory's *Dialogues* under the king's inspiration. The impulse towards reform came, at length, from the Benedictines, and was fully developed during the reign of Edgar (959–975). Though its origin dates back to the fifth century, the Benedictine reform failed to reach England before the tenth century. Insisting, as it did, upon the regular performance of the liturgy, upon daily study, and manual labour, the *Benedictine Code* had rapidly changed the face of things upon the Continent, and, under Æðelwold, its influence spread from Fleury to Winchester and Abingdon. Dilapidated foundations were restored, secular monks expelled, and *scriptoria* established throughout the country. Somewhat earlier, under Dunstan, reforms had been introduced at Glastonbury, not only in the study of letters but in the fine arts generally,—Church music, embroidery, smithwork, and metal-casting. But Dunstan's efforts were largely isolated, and the organisation of reform was left to his successor. Under Ædelwold, the study of grammar and poetry was pursued with vigour, he himself supplying a free translation of the famous *Code*, together with an account of the history of the Church in England.

After Ælfred, the most important figure in Old English literary history is Ælfric. His relation to the reform movement is clearly seen from the fact that he was a pupil of Ædelwold, who had himself studied under Dunstan. Born *c.* 955, Ælfric was educated at Winchester, whence he removed, in 987, to Cerne (or Cernel) in Dorsetshire. In 1005, he became abbot at Eynsham, and died there *c.* 1025. Ælfric's *Homilies* were composed at Cerne : they had been anticipated, but in a different way, by the Blickling series. These latter had covered the period from Christmas to Pentecost, concluding with legendary accounts of John the Baptist, Peter and Paul, Sts. Martin, Michael, and Andrew. In comparison with the more refined method of Ælfric, their style appears homely ; legendary material abounds, together with a certain happy intrusion of poetic matter, derived largely from the sources. For example, St. Martin offers half his cloak to a poor man, and, on the following night, sees the Christ clad in the same garment, St. Paul has a vision of the souls of the wicked, clinging to a cliff, which rises above a dark pool, filled with sea-beasts, and so on. Ælfric viewed the ecclesiastical legends in a critical spirit, adopting a plain and direct exegesis, with explanations of foreign names and references to incidents of daily life. His *Homilies* fall into two series, dated, on the evidence of the dedication to Archbishop Sigeric, *c.* 991 and 994. Forty homilies, including interpretations of the Paternoster and Creed, together with accounts of John the

Baptist, Laurentius, Bartholomew, Michael, Clement, and Andrew, constitute the first series, the sources being indicated in the preliminary address. The English preface, added later, explains how Ælfric afterwards translated the whole material into the vernacular for the benefit of unlearned men :

Then it ran in my mind, I trust through God's grace, that I would translate the book from Latin into English, not from the assurance of much learning but because I saw and heard much folly in many English books, which ignorant men innocently reckoned as wise : and I grieved that they neither knew nor possessed gospel teachings in their writings, save those alone who knew Latin, and those books excepted which Ælfred the king wisely turned from Latin into English, which are to be had.

In the second series of forty-five, homilies upon the Nativity, Palm Sunday, and the efficacy of the Holy Mass appear side by side with accounts of Gregory the Great, the Invention of the Holy Cross, and the Seven Sleepers. The two series, each originally of forty discourses and associated with particular Sundays and Feast Days, were designed for instruction in doctrinal matters and ecclesiastical history. The tendency to overstrain interpretation is shared by Ælfric with his contemporaries, but there are enlightened passages, such as the following from the Mid-Lent Sunday discourse (1st series) :

God hath wrought many miracles and daily works ; but the miracles are much weakened in men's sight, because they are very usual. It is a greater miracle that God Almighty every day feeds all the world, and directs the good, than that miracle that he filled five thousand men with five loaves.

The ornateness of the language, with its care for rhythm and alliteration,

Fela wundra worhte God, and dæghwamlice wyrcð,

marks an advance upon Ælfred : at the same time, the

E.L.C.   E

manner is sympathetic and in touch with its audience. In other homilies, however, Ælfric drew more largely upon these adventitious aids, and in the *Saints' Lives*, 996–997, his rhythm comes perilously near to that of verse.

Ælfric's two text-books, the *Latin Grammar* and the *Colloquy*, appear to have been written immediately after the *Homilies*. The *Grammar*, based upon Donatus and the *Institutiones Grammaticæ* of Priscian, is followed in some MSS. by a *Latin-English Glossary*. More interesting is the *Colloquy*, accompanied in MS. Tiberius A. 3 by an interlinear translation. The form is that of the dialogue, introducing the pupil to the various functions of the estates of the realm. In this way, Ælfric inaugurated a new and direct method of instruction in both language and general knowledge :

> Hwylcne cræft canst þu ?
> M. Qualem artem scis tu ?
> Ic eom fiscere
> P. Ego sum piscator
> Hwæt begytst þu of þinum cræfte ?
> M. Quid adquiris de tua arte ?
> Bigleofan, and scrud, and feoh.
> P. Victum, et vestitum, et pecuniam.
> Hu gefehst þu fiscas ?
> M. Quomodo capis pisces ?
> Ic astigie min scip, and wyrpe max mine on ea, and
> P. Conscendo navem, et pono retia mea in amne, et
> angil (æs) ic wyrpe and spyrtan, and swa hwæt swa
> hamum projicio   et sportas   et quicquid
> hig gehæfta   ic gemine
> ceperint   sumo

Ælfric's translations from the Bible bear an intimate relationship to his homiletic work : the versions are free, with large omissions. The task was not completed, and we have only portions of the *Pentateuch*, of *Joshua*, and *Judges* from his pen. He states, however, that he had been engaged upon other books, namely *Kings, Daniel, Job, Esther,* and the apocryphal *Judith.* The alliterative style connects these versions with the *Saints' Lives.* Along with the *Rushworth,* the *Lindisfarne,* and the *West Saxon versions of the Gospels,* they represent a preliminary attempt to provide Englishmen with a vernacular rendering of the various portions of the Bible. Somewhat later, Ælfric wrote a *Treatise on the Old and New Testaments,* summarising the various books, and, thus, providing an interesting introduction to the study of the Bible, in general.

In addition to these works on a large scale, Ælfric contributed a *Life of Aedelwold,* translations of the *Hexameron* of Basil and of Bede's *De Temporibus,* besides a number of detached letters and homilies. Among these latter, the *Pastoral letter* to Bishop Wulfsige attracted attention during the Reformation period, Ælfric being claimed as a follower of Ratramnus in his spiritual conception of the Eucharist. His *Easter Homily* also took rank among the more important of theological pronouncements :

Whatsoever there is in the housel, which gives us the substance of life, arises from its ghostly power and invisible efficacy.

Ælfric ranks, accordingly, as a theologian of distinction, second only to his position as a cultured representative of letters.

The *Homilies* of Wulfstan, bishop of York and Worcester betray a fiery indignation, prompted by the evils of Æðelred's reign. Not more than half-a-dozen, perhaps, are authentic, but, among these, the famous *Sermo Lupi ad Anglos* occupies the central position. In his employment of poetic devices Wulfstan went beyond Ælfric, and his alliteration, assonance, and end-rhyme suggest kinship with contemporary ballads :

Ne dohte hit nū lange inne ne ūte, ac wæs here and hunger, bryne and blōdgyte, on gewelhwylcon ende oft and gelōme ;

and ūs stalu and cwalu, strīc and steorfa, orfcwealm and uncoðu, hōl and hete, and rȳpera rēaflāc, derede swȳðe ðearle, and ūs ungylda swȳðe gedrehton, and ūs unwedera for-oft wēoldan unwæstma.

During the later Anglo-Saxon period, there appeared a number of scientific treatises, belonging to the class of leech-books, herbalries, and lapidaries, the most general being the *Handbook* of Byrhtferð, with dissertations upon chronology, the ages of the world, grammar, metre, and rhetoric. A counterpart to *Salomon and Marcolf* appeared in the dialogue of *Adrian and Ritheus*, while, late in the twelfth century, came a translation of the *Elucidarium*. The marvels of the East were reflected in Alexander's *Letter to Aristotle* and the *Wonders of the East*. Lastly, a venture in romance, the story of *Apollonius of Tyre* (eleventh century), links the Anglo-Saxon period, through the intermediary of Gower and Lawrence Twine, with Shakespeare, who drew upon the story in *Pericles*.

PART II
THE MIDDLE ENGLISH PERIOD

XI. RELIGIOUS LITERATURE

HOMILIES, LEGENDS, AND DIDACTIC PIECES

The religious literature of the Middle English period is most clearly related to that of its predecessor in the department of the sermon or homily. In accordance with the precedent provided by writers like Bede and Ælfric, the earliest examples of Middle English homily group themselves into series, distinguished by the names of the particular MSS., in which they occur. Thus, we have from the twelfth century the so-called Bodley, Lambeth, and Trinity homilies, followed, somewhat later, by the Cotton Vespasian and the Kentish. In particular instances, Ælfric's discourses are simply retold, and there is a general obligation to writers like Augustine, Jerome, and Isidore. The employment of *exempla* is not usual in these early collections, though there is a considerable amount of quaint material, such as the fable of the crab and the account of Paul's descent into Hell (Lambeth), and the illustration from the natural history of the adder (Trinity). The tendency to indulge in speculative etymologies is in accordance with the practice of Isidore. On the whole, the exegesis is healthy and thorough, though little attempt is made to relate it to contemporary conditions. A crude type of symbolism appears in the discourse on the miracle of Cana (Kentish), where the water is identified with the cold Christian and the wine with the love of God. The Cotton Vespasian collection is distinguished by the occurrence of a pretty allegory concerning a king who, having made an experiment to distinguish friends from foes, proceeded to reward them according to their deserts. This so-called *Bispel* is one of the best things in the prose of the early Middle English period. A curious interest attaches to the verse-piece, entitled *A lutel soth sermun*. It is composed, with occasional variation, in four-line stanzas rhyming abcb, and portrays the ill-condition of the times. The preacher denounces chapmen, bakers, and brewers, who deceive their customers, and then, turning to the young men and maidens of his day, comments particularly upon their behaviour in Church and the market-place :

> At chireche and at chepyng
> Hwanne heo togadere come
> Heo runeþ togaderes
> And spekeþ of derne luue.
> Hwenne heo to chirche cumeþ
> To þon holy daye
> Eueruych wile his leof iseo
> þer yef he may,
> Heo biholdeþ Watekin
> Mid swiþe gled eye.

The apocryphal matter in the *Homilies* is but a sign of the times, and its vogue may be illustrated from a number of detached treatises belonging, for the most part, to the thirteenth and fourteenth centuries. Chief among these are the fanciful accounts of the early life of the Saviour, known as the *Birth of Jesus* and the *Childhood of Jesus* and extant in several versions. The former, as represented by MS. Egerton 1993, introduces the Virgin as a daughter of Joachim and Anna, and describes her childhood and marriage. Then follow the events at Bethlehem, the visits of the shepherds and the Magi. The slaughter of the innocents leads up to the flight into Egypt, and, *en route*, occurs the miracle of the tree. The idols fall in Egypt in the presence of the divine child. The Holy Family returns to Palestine, while Jesus is left in Jerusalem. The crude legends of the sparrows formed of clay, of the game of leap-frog, in which several Jewish children were killed, of the pitcher hung from a sunbeam, etc., appear, side by side with the Egyptian wonders, in the Lauderdale version (MS. 108). For this varied material a general source lay to hand in the apocryphal *Infancy* and the *Birth of Mary*. Parallel pieces are the *Assumption of Our Lady* and the accounts of Judas and Pilate in the *Southern Legendary Collection*. There is a romantic version of the two latter in *Titus and Vespasian* : further, a ballad in MS. Camb. Trin. Coll. B. 14–39, which provides Judas with a sister, who counsels him ill :

> Judas, þou were wrþe me stende þe with ston
> For the false prophete þet tou bilevest upon.

In his sleep, Judas loses thirty pieces of silver, and, thus, acquires a motive for his bargain with Pilate :

> I nul sulle my Loverd for nones cunnes eiȝte
> Bote hit be for þe þritte platten þat he me bitaiȝte.

A variant of the story of Joseph of Arimathea, the *Holy Blood of Hayles* (fifteenth century), recounts how Joseph, after receiving the sacred blood in a vessel, was imprisoned for forty-two years :

> þerin he was two and fowrty ȝere
> Aftyr oure lorde dyed upon þe tre
> Wyt þat blode fayre and clere
> þat hym sustened wele in euere degre.

During the siege of Jerusalem, Joseph was discovered in prison, but fell dead, immediately the blood was removed from him. Together with the vernicle and other relics, the holy blood was transferred to Rome, whence Charlemagne carried a portion to Germany, another being brought to England, to the Abbey of Hayles, founded by the Earl of Cornwall. Chief among Old Testament legends are the *Canticum de Creatione* and the prose lives of *Adam and Eve*, which relate, with much material in common, the stories of the Fall, the expulsion from Paradise, Seth's return thereto, and the committing

of Adam's life to tablets of stone. The Vernon account
may be taken as representative. It opens with a fantastic
account of the origin of the name Adam from the initial
letters of the four stars, Anatalim, Dysus, Arcis, and
Messembrion. The North and East of Paradise were,
afterwards, assigned to Adam, the South and West to
Eve. After their expulsion, the pair appeared clothed
in skins of beasts, betokening that their offspring should
die in earth. Adam underwent penance in the water of
Jordan, Eve in the Tigris, where she was, once more,
tempted. Cain slew Abel with the cheek-bone of an ass,
and was banished together with his wife, Calmana. Eve,
thereupon, set out for Paradise to secure the oil of mercy,
accompanied by Seth. After Adam's death, Seth placed
the grains of an apple under his father's tongue, whence
sprang the three shoots, on which Christ died. The
tablets, upon which the history of Adam was recounted,
were discovered after the Deluge, and came eventually
into the hands of Solomon, who interpreted them. The
legends of the *Holy Rood* carry on the history of the Cross
to the date of its discovery by Helena, the materials being
accessible in the *Bodley History*, the *Cursor Mundi*, and
the Northern and Southern Legendary collections.
After the finding of the Cross, Judas was baptised under
the name of Ciriacus (Quiriacus), and ended his career
in martyrdom.

The interesting section of Vision literature had been
inaugurated by Bede's accounts of Furseus and of
Drihthelm. In the latter, purgatory figured as a place
where cold and heat alternate, "on the left it appeared
full of dreadfull flames, the other side was no less horrid
for violent hail and cold snow, flying in all directions."
Then followed visions of hell and of heaven, the latter
divided into two areas, reserved respectively for the
souls of the righteous and of those less perfect. In the
thirteenth century appeared the *Vision of St. Paul*,
expanded in the Vernon text of the fourteenth century.
Paul and Michael had visited the souls in hell and wit-

nessed the cruel ingenuity of their torments—the burning trees, the heated cauldron, the revolving wheel, the lake of reptiles, the boiling pitch, etc. Their pity was moved, and, in response to their prayers, a respite from Saturday to Monday in each week was secured for the tormented. Still more horrible were the tortures, catalogued in the *Vision of Tundale*, a highly popular piece existing in Latin, French, German, Italian, and Icelandic, as well as in English. Further, visions were related of Thurkill and the Monk of Evesham, the latter distinguished by an account of a theatrical performance, in which the damned conduct an entertainment for the amusement of the fiends. The elaborate and interesting *St. Patrick's Purgatory* recounts how Owayne Miles discovered a pit leading to purgatory. He was dragged by fiends to a spot, where men and women were bound naked to the ground and tortured by fire. In other places, adders gnawed them, nails pierced their sides, brimstone and chains tormented them : some were roasted on gridirons, hung up by awls thrust through their eyes, spitted like geese, or fastened to a reeking wheel. At length, Owayne was taken to the pit of hell, whence he passed out, by Christ's help, over a narrow bridge. He arrived at a place of sweet smelling spices, where a fair light shone, this latter region being identified with Paradise.

A further link with the Anglo-Saxon period may be found in the extensive department of the *Saints' Lives*. To this type Cynewulf had devoted most of his energies and provided models, to which, in point of artistry, the new period could with difficulty attain. His legends were, however, detached, and it was not till after the Council of Tours, in the ninth century, that the habit arose of combining legends into cycles, as in the *Blickling Homilies* and the *Saints' Lives* of Ælfric. The twelfth and thirteenth centuries were the flourishing period of the Saint's Life, the significant fact in its history being its triumph over the homilies, which were slowly ousted from the Saints' days, and confined to the regular offices

of the ecclesiastical year.   Gradually, legendary matter
was introduced into the *temporale* itself, and the need
for organised material led to the compilation, at the end
of the thirteenth century, of two great native series, the
Northern and the Southern *Legendaries*.   Such under-
takings were stimulated by the appearance (*c.* 1260–
1270) of Jacobus de Voragine's famous book, the *Legenda
Aurea*—itself a compilation from various sources.   Meantime, the detached Saint's Life had continued to be
written with some success, and we possess, from the
beginning of the thirteenth century, three alliterative
prose lives of St. Margaret, St. Juliana, and St. Katherine,
other versions of which were destined to appear in later
collections.   Of the former, there is an interesting variant
in stanzas, dated *c.* 1270 :   there is, also, a tail-rhymed
version of the life of St. Eustace, a figure familiar to
romance.   From the fourteenth century date interesting
accounts of St. Gregory and Mary Magdalene, followed,
in the fifteenth century, by Theophilus and Christopher.
The *Lives of the Saints* suffer, in general, from a monotony
of handling :   prodigies of heroism are performed in the
face of excruciating tortures, and there is much exag-
geration in the incidents, as, for example, in *St. Anasthasia*.
But, after all, there is considerable variety of story, from
the account of St. Thomas of India to that of St. Nicholas,
together with an abundance of folk-lore, humour, and
piety.   The Gregory legend has the same kind of interest
as the romances—the exposure of a child of obscure birth,
his adventures by land and sea, and his final triumph
over all obstacles—together with much charm of detail :

> þe ffisscheres seiden boþe iliche
> þe abbot heo onswereden sone
> Bi Jesu Kyng of heuene riche
> Ur þinges beþ þerinne idone
> Wiþ þat þe child bigon to skrike
> Wiþ steuene as hit were a grome
> þe ffisschers wenden to han ben a swike
> Heo ne wusten what to done.

þe abbot bad hem wiþouten wouh
Undo þe tonne þat he þer seyh
þe ffisschers were redi inouȝ
To don his wille þat ilke day
A cloþ of selk þe abbot updrouh
þat on þe child in þe cradel lay
þo lay þe luytel child and louh
Uppon þe abbot wiþ eȝen gray.

Attractions of another kind, due to a variety of sources, characterise the *Theophilus*, the *Christopher*, and *Mary Magdalene*, while *St. Brandan* is unique in its combination of the spirit of adventure with the atmosphere of the Celtic other-world.

The attempt, inaugurated in the Anglo-Saxon period, to provide vernacular renderings of the Scriptures was continued, at the end of the thirteenth century, in the *Surtees Psalter*. In West Midland of the same period a prose version appeared, consisting of the whole of the Psalms, eleven Canticles, and the Athanasian Creed. The dialect material of the *Surtees Psalter* is interesting, though its range of appeal must necessarily have been limited :

Louand Lauerd calle sal I,
And fra mi faas be sauf for-thi.
Umgaf me sorwes of dede ;
Umgriped me weeles of quede.

The dominance of allegory in the department of religious literature is illustrated by the *Castle of Love* of Bishop Grosseteste, of which there were, at least, three Middle English versions. The castle, girt with the towers of the cardinal virtues, the baillies of maidenhood, chastity, and wedlock, and the barbicans of the seven virtues, represents the Virgin. Altogether, the poem constitutes an attractive piece of symbolism. Less happy in the handling of its theme was the prose *Abbey of the Holy Ghost*, its successor in the fourteenth century.

The first important religious poem of the new period,

the *Poema Morale*, appeared, in the southern dialect, towards the close of the twelfth century. The author possibly belonged to the district, bounded by the Avon and the Stour, an inference drawn from one of his illustrations. His poem partakes of the nature of a warning and of an appeal. With considerable vividness he describes the pains of Hell,—its hunger and thirst, its heat and cold, its adders and snakes,—to contrast them with a vision of Heaven, spiritually conceived :

> Ne sceal ðer beon ne bried ne win ne oðer cunnes este,
> God ane sceal beo eche lif end blisse end eche reste.

The poet shows himself a wise counsellor, with knowledge derived from experience. Age has mellowed him, and he is ready to dispense advice. His personality still attracts, and he cannot have been without influence on his early circle of readers. The *Poema Morale* does not betray a strong intellect, but we are conscious of the author's insight and sincerity. His language is simple, and his syntax almost modern. Of poetical flights he has none, though the metaphor in which the unregenerate are described as " striving against the hill " is a happy augury of possible things. The conceptions of the " mansions above " is, also, suggestive of an intellect capable of emancipation.

The metre represents an extremely early attempt to naturalise the Latin septenar, the rhythm being trochaic, or iambic, according as the initial unaccented syllable is, or is not, suppressed. In its second variety, this metre is identical with that of Orm, but the poet has gone further than his successor in the employment of end-rhyme. The following example from the Egerton MS. (one of seven extant MSS.) will serve to illustrate his rhythm, and, at the same time, a passing mood, his interest in the terminology of the forbidden paradise of Romance :

> Ne sceal ðer beo fah ne græi ne kuning ne ermine
> ne aquierne ne martres cheole ne beuer ne sabeline

Ne sceal der beo sciet ne scrud ne woruld wele nane
eal þe murhde þe me us bihat al hit sceal beo god ane.

The monitory tone of the *Poema Morale* characterises
a whole group of poems, composed upon the text, Memento
homo quod cinis es et in cinerem reverteris. Of these,
Erthe upon Erthe has retained its popularity down to
modern times, being frequently drawn upon for head-
stones and mural inscriptions. In general, its theme is
akin to those of the *Soul and the Body* and the *Dance of
Death*, but, despite the bilingual character of MS. Harleian
913, its *provenance* appears to be English. At least
three versions exist, the nucleus being, perhaps, the
following stanza from MS. Harleian 2253 :

> Erþe toc of erþe erþe wyþ woh,
> Erþe oþer erþe to þe erþe droh,
> Erþe leyde erþe in erþene þroh,
> þo heuede erþe of erþe erþe ynoh.

The related *Sayings of St. Bernard*, the *Song on Death*,
Old Age, and *Maximian* enforce their warnings in different
ways, though the caprices of Fortune, the decay of the
physical powers, and the horrors of the grave are treated
by all with evident interest. Thus, the little poem on
Old Age (MS. Harl. 913) handles its theme with gusto,
in a curious mixture of alliterative and rhyming lines.
With a larger canvas at his disposal, the author of
Maximian has added a contrasted picture of youth :
the old man, avoided by friends and relatives alike,
exults in the fact that he was once fair as Absalom :

> Ase I rod thourh Rome,
> Richest alre home,
> > With murthes as ycholde,
> Ledys wyht so swon,
> Maidnes shene so bon,
> > Me come to bi-holde :
> Ant seyden on after on,
> " ȝent ryd Maximon,
> > With is burnes bolde."

Nou nis non of the,
That wolleth me y-se
In mine clothes olde.

The *Ormulum* was the first important product of the
North-Midland area to appear after the Conquest, and
occupies a position, analogous to that of the *Brut* in the
South. It has been dated *c.* 1200. The author gives
his name in two forms as Orm and Ormin, for both of
which a Scandinavian origin may be suspected. He
informs us that he named his book after himself :

Thiss boc is nemmnedd Orrmulum
forrthi thatt Orrm itt wrohhte.

Orm's ecclesiastical position was that of an Augustinian
canon regular, and it is probable that he was connected
with Lincolnshire, where a number of Augustinian houses
existed in his day. The *Ormulum* is a metrical paraphrase of the Gospels for the year, accompanied by
interpretations and applications. It has come down to
us in fragmentary form, extending to some 10,000 lines,
but representing only about an eighth of the original
plan. The unique MS., described in a catalogue of 1666
as " an old Swedish or Gothic book on the Gospel," is
the author's holograph, with additions and corrections
in various hands. The *Ormulum* is of didactic intent,
and designed for the vulgar. In the *Dedication* to Walter,
Orm recalls the part played by his " brother " in originating the book :

Thu thohhtesst tatt itt mihhte wel till mikell frame turrnenn
Yif Ennglissh follc, forr lufe off Crist, itt wollde yerne lernenn.

This interest in the well-being of the folk constitutes
Orm's chief claim on our gratitude. At the risk of
becoming tedious, he reiterates his points, and the
doctrine he provides bears the stamp of orthodoxy :
for it is to Bede and Gregory, rather than to Anselm and
the new teachers, that he turns for his material. The
allegorical and mystical explanations and the curious

interest in proper names, like Amminadab, have a smack of pedantry about them, but, in this, Orm merely followed the footsteps of Isidore and earlier writers. Orm's metre is of great interest for the light it throws on the origin of our common metre, in one of its varieties. Its source was the Latin septenar, trochaic or iambic, found in mediæval students' songs, and elsewhere. Each line consists strictly of fifteen syllables, broken by the cæsura into sets of eights and sevens. Orm eschewed rhyme, so essential to his modern representatives, cf. the following passage from the *Holy Fair*:

> The risin' sun, owre Galston muirs,
> Wi' glorious light was glintin';
> The hares were hirplin' down the furrs,
> The lav'rocks they were chantin'.
>
> .   .   .   .   .

In spelling Orm was a purist, and his poem constitutes a precious document to the philologist. He distinguishes between three kinds of "g," (1) the explosive, (2) the continuant, and (3) the affricate, and, by his habit of doubling consonants after short vowels, enables us to ascertain vowel quantities. His dread of scribal errors is well illustrated by the following passage:

Annd whase wilenn shall thiss boc efft otherr sithe writenn,
Himm bidde icc thatt het write rihht, swa summ this boc
    himm taechethth,
All thwerrtut affterr thatt itt iss uppo thiss firrste bisne,
Withth all swillc rime alls her iss sett, withth all se fele wordess;
And tatt he loke wel thatt he an bocstaff write twiggess
Egg whaer thaer itt uppo thiss boc iss writenn o thatt wise.

The aim of the author of the *Ormulum* was religious enlightenment: the same is apparent in the prose treatises, the *Wooing of Our Lord, Holy Maidenhood,* and *Soul's Ward*, which bridge the interval between Orm's poem and *Genesis and Exodus* (c. 1250). All are written in a kind of alliterative prose, which imparts to them a measure of poetic refinement. The *Wooing of Our Lord*

E.L.C.   F

is a fine example of erotic mysticism, instinct with the tenderest emotion, but it is difficult for the modern mind to appreciate the rigorous asceticism, proclaimed by the author of *Holy Maidenhood*. An ingenious allegory forms the basis of the third piece, *Soul's Ward*, in some ways an early anticipation of the method of Bunyan's *Holy War*.

In verse, a *Good Orison of Our Lady* (c. 1210) introduces the cult of the Virgin, inherited from the twelfth-century mystics. The lines are irregular, and, alongside of the fourteener, we find possible anticipations of the alexandrine, if not of the decasyllable :

> þu ert mire soule liht and mine heorte blisse,
> mi lif and mi tohope, min heale mid iwisse.

But the metrical interest of the *Good Orison* is surpassed by that of *Genesis and Exodus*, a wonderful experiment in short rhyming couplets, with a preponderating number of monosyllabic endings. The main source was Comestor's *Historia Scholastica* (twelfth century), while some use was made of Philippe de Thaon's *Comput*. The author betrays no sympathy with the mystics, his purpose being to produce a concise paraphrase of the earlier books of the Old Testament, with, as little as possible, legendary matter. This didactic intent he carried out in a somewhat bald and uninspiring way, though his achievement was no slight one, having regard to chronology : the " small words " were inevitable in any attempt to popularise such material in " landes speech." An extract from the history of Moses will serve to illustrate, at one and the same time, the metrical advance and the fascination of legend for the mediæval mind :

> He bad ðis child brennen to colen
> And he toc is, hu migt he it ðolen ?
> And in hise muth so depe he is dede
> Hise tunges ende is brent ðormide ;
> ðorfore seide ðe ebru witterlike
> ðat he spac siðen miserlike.

At the outset of the fourteenth century, the work of religious instruction in verse was continued in an encyclopædic poem, the *Cursor Mundi* (c. 1320). In regular couplets of four stresses, the history of the Seven Ages is reviewed, some MSS. adding miscellaneous prayers and other material, at the close. The variety of the contents may be realised from the fact that the author includes, along with the Biblical story, material from the Rood-literature, the allegorico-religious poetry, the apocrypha, the Virgin poems, and the lives of the martyrs. His main source, was, however, the *Historia Scholastica* of Peter Comestor. The *Cursor Mundi* is, essentially, a popular book, with its material attractively manipulated. It represents an attempt to wean readers by imparting to religious instruction something of the attraction of romance.

The tendency to make verse the vehicle of instruction in general matters accounts for the rarity of prose during the thirteenth century ; in this respect, we have a curious parallel with the literary conditions of the age of Anne. The outstanding example of didactic religious prose, in this period, was the *Ancren Riwle*, extant in English, French, and Latin. Of these versions, Macaulay assigned the priority to the French, the Latin being regarded as a translation of the English ; but the drift of the evidence makes an English original certain. A note at the head of the Latin version (Magdalen Coll. Oxf. 67) assigns the authorship to Simon of Ghent, Bishop of Salisbury, who prepared it "sororibus suis Anachoritis apud Tarente." Richard Poore, Bishop of Chichester, Salisbury, and Durham, has, also, been claimed as the author, on the ground that he was born at Tarrent (Dorsetshire), and buried there in 1237. The claim of neither of these can, however, be substantiated. The *Ancren Riwle* is a treatise on the conduct of life, addressed to three recluses who had retired to an anchor-hold, in close proximity to a church. The author distinguishes carefully between what he regards as the " outward " and

the "inward rule." Being no formalist, he lays the
greater stress on the latter, but, as regards the former,
counsels adhesion to the rule of St. James, according to
which " Pure religion and undefiled before God and the
Father is this, To visit the fatherless and widows in their
affliction, and to keep himself unspotted from the world."
In the same way, he limits the anchoresses' vows to those
of obedience, chastity and constancy. The *Ancren
Riwle* is a liberal and kindly tractate, with much variety
of material. The vivid account of the Seven Deadly
Sins supplies a pendant to those in *Piers Plowman*, the
Handlyng Synne, the *Ayenbite of Inwyt*, and the *Parson's
Tale* :

The wrathful man fences with knives before the devil :
he is the devil's knife-thrower, and plays with swords, and
bears them by the sharp point upon his tongue.

Following upon this comes the charming allegory,
known as the " Wooing of Our Lord," one of the tenderest
things in mediaeval prose, and a testimony to the pre-
valence of erotic mysticism. The concluding section,
" Of domestic matters," interests by its detail and
occasional *naïveté*. The dress and daily occupation of
the anchoresses are considered, in turn. They are to
concern themselves as little as possible with outside
affairs. An anchoress must not be a buyer nor a seller.
The sewing of church vestments and of garments for
the poor will provide legitimate employment. Two
maids may be kept, one as an " out-sister." During
the greater part of the day silence should be observed,
but rigorous penance is discountenanced. The thumb-
nail sketches from familiar life greatly enhance the
charm of the book,—the pedlar selling his soap, Slurry,
the kitchen-boy, insulting the maids while he washes
the dishes, and the tender account of the child, cited in
illustration of the " comfort of the Lord " :

Our Lord when he suffers us to be tempted, plays with
us as the mother with her darling : she flies from him, and

hides herself, and leaves him to sit alone, and look timidly round, and call ' Dame ! dame ! ' and weep a while : then she leaps forth laughing with open arms, and embraces and kisses him and wipes his eyes.

A snatch of popular song, " My eye is ever toward the sheltering wood, wherein is he I love," contrasts with the learned citations from Jerome, Augustine, Benedict, Anselm, and Bernard of Clairvaux, with which the book is liberally bestrewn.

XII. THE ORGANISATION OF ROMANCE

(a) THE MATTER OF FRANCE.

The classification of mediæval romance presents considerable difficulties, though certain groups are easily distinguishable, and were, indeed, recognized, as far back as the twelfth century, by the *trouvère*, Jean Bodel :

Ne sont que trois matières a nul home attendant
De France et de Bretaigne et de Rome la grant.

Of these " matters " so-called, that of France may be accorded its traditional priority, though it cannot claim to have, at any time, assumed first-rate interest in the eyes of Englishmen.

Under the title of *chanson de geste*, the epic was the favourite branch of poetry, cultivated in France during the mediæval period. At first concerned with the deeds of a single hero, the *chanson* extended its scope so as to embrace the history of a whole family, and, finally, degenerated into the prose " jest-book " of the later Middle Ages.

The origin of the *chanson de geste* has been sought in

popular songs or *cantilènes*, of the fifth to the ninth centuries, the existence of which has been deduced from references in Gregory of Tours, Fredegarius, and later chroniclers.

Quorum quia vulgata sunt nomina dicere supersedi,

so writes the biographer of Louis with reference to the heroes of Roncesvalles. But recent criticism, represented by M. Bédier, assigns the *chansons de geste* exclusively to the eleventh century, and associates their formation with religious festivals, fairs, pilgrimages, etc. They derive from the clerks, and not from popular inspiration. Still, M. Bédier admits that the *chansons* can scarcely be regarded as a *proles sine matre creata*, and it is probable that certain folk-lore, as well as metrical, characteristics derive from popular ballads of an earlier period. The possibility that the Norman inroads of the ninth and tenth centuries may have inspired contemporary songs, afterwards embodied in the epics, has also been urged.

In their extant forms, the *chansons de geste* represent a period, extending from the end of the eleventh well into the fourteenth century. They number roughly eighty, and fall into groups of varying denomination, the chief being : (1) the *geste* of the king (represented by *Roland, Mainet, Otinel, Fierabras*, etc.) ; (2) the *geste* of the traitors (*Doon de Mayence, Renaud de Montauban, Raoul de Cambrai*, etc.) ; (3) the *geste* of William (*Aliscans, Aimeri de Narbonne*, etc.). In the earliest *chansons*, lines were grouped into *laisses* of varying length, in which assonance assumed the function of rhyme. The line itself consisted of ten syllables, divided into 4's and 6's, or *vice-versâ*, by the cæsura. An extra unaccented syllable was permissible before the cæsura, and, similarly, at the end. Later on, the decasyllabic line was displaced by one of twelve syllables, and assonance by rhyme. The *chansons* were the work of *trouvères*, and intended for recitation. The prose versions are of late date, and betray considerable rehandling of the materials.

Outside France, the Charlemagne legends attained to much vogue. In Italy, at the beginning of the fifteenth century, appeared a *rifacimento* of chivalrous legend, under the title, *Reali di Francia*, while Ariosto, in the sixteenth century, paid a direct compliment to the spell of Roland in his *Orlando Furioso*. In Spain, the *Cronica* of Alfonso X contained, in its third section, an account of Charlemagne and Roncesvalles, which was influential in developing a native heroic cycle. Germany, in the thirteenth century, produced in *Karl* and *Karl Mainet* adaptations of *chansons*, particularly concerned with Charlemagne, while *Aliscans* was translated by Wolfram von Eschenbach, under the title of *Willehalm*. The great Norse compilation, the *Karlamagnussaga*, was based partly upon the *Pseudo-Turpin*, partly upon the *chansons* themselves.

In England, the vogue of the Charlemagne legends was considerable, but the quality of the versions was never first-rate. The famous *Chanson de Roland* has peculiar associations with England. The best MS. is preserved at Oxford, and a second at Trinity College, Cambridge. Further, as Wace tells us, the heroes of Roncesvalles formed the theme of Taillefer's song at Hastings, in 1066 :

> Devant le duc alout chantant
> De Karlemaigne e de Rolant
> E d'Olivier e des vassals
> Qui moururent en Rencevals.

A fragmentary version of the French poem survives from the end of the fourteenth century, in the S.W. Midland dialect. Compared with existing French MSS., this *Song of Roland* represents a very free translation : its exact source is, probably, yet to be discovered. The workmanship is rough-hewn, the author displaying command of neither rhyme nor metre.

Five English romances link themselves together as component parts of a great cycle, beginning with Charles' journey to the East and ending with Roncesvalles. These are *Roland and Vernagu*, the *Sege of Melayne*, *Otuel*, *Duke*

Rowlande and Sir Ottuell of Spayne, and the lost Fillingham *Otuel* (so named from its former owner). The poems
are of various dialects, metres and dates, and represent
the work of several authors. In the opening section
(*Roland and Vernagu*), Charles is summoned to the East
to aid Constantine against the Saracens. Having secured
certain precious relics there, among which were the holy
crown, the arm of St. Simeon, our Lady's smock, and one
of the nails, he made his way to Spain and started on a
triumphal progress, culminating in Galicia, where he
founded a church in honour of St. James. One day, while
he held his court, a giant, Vernagu, entered and challenged
the knights to single combat. His treatment of those who
presented themselves was highly contemptuous but, at
length,

> Rouland with Durindale
> Brewe him miche bale.

During the adjournment of the fight, Roland magnani-
mously assisted the giant's sleep by placing a stone under
his head for a pillow. Roland discussed Christian
theology with Vernagu, but to no purpose :

> Quoth Vernagu, " now ich wot
> ȝour cristen lawe eueri grot
> Now we wil fight.
> Whether lawe better be
> Sone we schul yse,
> Long ar it be night.

The fight was renewed and Roland killed the giant. In
the second section (*Sege of Melayne*), Charles sent an army
to the relief of Milan under the leadership of Roland, who
was captured, along with Oliver and Guy of Burgundy.
The failure of the expedition was set down to Ganelon's
treachery. Escaping, at length, to Paris the knights
looked for vengeance, but Ganelon, gaining Charles' ear,
interfered with their plans once more. Charles' reluct-
ance to act angered Turpin, who proceeded to excom-
municate him. In the subsequent campaign, Turpin

played a hero's part, performing prodigies of valour, and swearing never to eat nor drink until Milan was taken. *Otuel* is linked to the preceding sections by a reference at the close of *Roland and Vernagu*. Otuel represented King Garcy of Lombardy, from whom he brought a message to Charles, bidding him renounce Christianity. He displayed great courage, in face of the French knights. As a nephew of Vernagu, it was Roland he was anxious to meet. The combat took place, and, during its course, Roland offered Otuel the hand of Belisant. Otuel accepted, and was converted, simultaneously. In the latter part of the romance, Otuel aided the French knights against Garcy, who submitted, at length. The story of Otuel was retold in the fourth section (*Duke Rowlande and Sir Ottuel*), with large variations. Finally, the Fillingham *Otuel* (as described by Ellis) recounted Charles' campaign against Ibrahim of Seville, and his victory over the king of Navarre, concluding with an account of Ganelon's treachery and the final disaster at Roncesvalles.

An examination of the romances makes it clear that this cycle so-called lacks sequence. Apart from defects in the MSS., the romances are complete in themselves. Further, the ground, covered by *Duke Rowlande*, is that of its predecessor, while the Fillingham *Otuel* introduces once again that Ibrahim of Spain, who figured at the outset of *Roland and Vernagu*. We have, therefore, merely a rough summary, with omissions and repetitions, of the chief events of Charles' reign. The motive at the back of the romances, the attempt to magnify the importance of the Church, is clearly discernible. Miracles are of regular occurrence, while the part played by Turpin is not without significance. Charles himself is depicted from varying points of view, for, while he figures in *Roland and Vernagu* as a vigorous knight, twenty feet in height, with black hair and a ruddy complexion, in the *Sege of Melayne* he plays a sorry part over against Turpin.

Roland and Vernagu corresponds, generally, to the *Descriptio qualiter Carolus Magnus clavum et coronum*

Domini . . ., a Latin poem of the eleventh century, and to the *Pseudo-Turpin*. Vernagu's resolve to settle the rival 'claims of the two religions by combat is thus expressed in the latter :

"Tali igitur pacto," inquit Ferracutus, "tecum pugnabo ; quod si vera est hæc fides quam asseris, ego victus sim ; et si mendax est, tu victus sis ; et sit genti victæ iugiter opprobrium, victoribus autem laus et decus in aevum."

A comparison with the extract from *Roland and Vernagu*, cited above, will show that the English version is not based directly upon the Latin, and there is reason to believe that our author followed a French text. A French source may, also, be assumed for the *Sege of Melayne*. Both *Otuel* and its successor follow the *chanson*, known as *Otinel*, though the second runs much closer to the extant text. Finally, the *Pseudo-Turpin* provides the nearest analogue for the material in the Fillingham version.

The *Sowdone of Babylon* and *Sir Ferumbras* constitute another group, linked by the figure of Ferumbras. The introductory matter, in the *Sowdone*, relates how Laban of Babylon attacked Rome, assisted by Lukafer of Baldas, a suitor for the hand of his daughter, Floripas. During the interval between the summoning and the arrival of Charles, Ferumbras, the Sultan's son, unhorsed the Pope, the Saracens entered Rome, and the relics were removed. The main portion of the narrative corresponds generally with *Sir Ferumbras*, the central figure being Floripas, whose love for Guy of Burgundy caused her to exert herself, to the full, on behalf of the French knights. This section abounds in vigorous fighting and thrilling adventure. The material is of a highly popular character, as in the incident of the scorching of Naymes' beard, avenged by the burning of his assailant. The character of Floripas, likewise, displays crude elements. Curiously enough, the author of the *Sowdone* has attempted to combine with his matter an occasional imitation of

Chaucer, e.g. the description of spring and the incident of Floripas in the garden. From the metrical point of view, *Sir Ferumbras* is the more interesting, with its long rhyming couplets and irregular alliteration. Variation in the details suggests that the two romances represent different texts of the French *Fierabras*, though the opening of the *Sowdone* is related to the *Destruction de Rome*.

Ferumbras was, until quite recently, a familiar name throughout Britain and the Continent, and the reference in Barbour's *Bruce* attests his early popularity in Scotland.

In the fifteenth century, the famous *Huon of Bordeaux*, following its French original into the strange paths of Oriental marvel, prepared the way for the faery element in the *Midsummer Night's Dream*.

(b) THE MATTER OF BRITAIN.

Unlike Charlemagne, Arthur has always been a familiar figure to Englishmen, a fact for which many explanations might be adduced. In the first place, the proximity of the Celtic borderland made him, at the outset, a more or less accessible theme for poets ; his exploitation by the French and by the Norman conquerors of Britain was a factor of even greater importance ; again, the breadth of the theme itself, with its chivalry and its passion, its emancipation from convention, its adventurous incident and its mysticism—these elements, separately or combined, have made a continuous appeal to Englishmen, from the twelfth to the nineteenth century.

An attempt to assign to Arthur his position in history and legend would necessitate an examination of many literatures, Celtic, Germanic, and Romance. Even for our present purposes, it is impossible to ignore this material altogether, though the survey must necessarily be brief and limited to definite points of view.

The historicity of Arthur has been much debated, but without definite results. The Welsh evidence fails to carry us far, for, already in Nennius (c. A.D. 800), in the

oldest poems, and in the prose tales, Arthur has attracted
to himself an accretion of myth.   Nennius, indeed, speaks
of him as *dux bellorum*, which is taken to imply that, in
the defence of Britain against the Saxons, Arthur held
the rank of *Comes Britanniæ*.   A list of twelve battles,
in which the king participated, is added by Nennius,
the most famous of which, that of Mons Badonis, had
already been recorded by Gildas (sixth century) as having
taken place in the year of his own nativity (*c.* 500).
The absence of reference to Arthur in the *Anglo-Saxon
Chronicle* and in Bede has aroused suspicion, but it is
unnecessary to have recourse to a purely mythological
explanation of his origin, in view of the euhemeristic
arguments, urged in defence of other figures of epic and
romance.

Already in early Welsh literature accounts of Arthur
assumed a romantic cast, though many elements in the
primitive legend fail of a place in later forms, as known
to English literature.   From the outset, Arthur was the
husband of Gwenhywfar (Guinevere), and in close com-
panionship with Bedwyr (Bedivere) and Kei (Kay).
Associated with him, at a later period, were Peredur
(Perceval) and Gereint (Geraint).   Arthur conducted a
campaign against the Romans, slaying the Emperor in
single combat.   He fell in the battle of Camlan, in
consequence of Medraut's (Mordred) treachery, and was
buried in the isle of Avallach (Avallon).   A familiar
element, reproduced by Geoffrey, occurs already in
Nennius, who states that, at the battle of Guinnion,
Arthur bore the image of the Holy Virgin, mother of God,
upon his shoulders, and, through the power of our Lord
Jesus Christ and the holy Mary, put the Saxons to flight,
pursuing them the whole day with great slaughter.   The
position assigned to Arthur among the Christian worthies
finds an early justification here.   Unfamiliar features
occur, however, as early as the *Mirabilia*, associated with
Nennius, where Arthur is described as hunting the Porcus
Troit, accompanied by his famous hound, Cabal : another

version of this story appeared later in *Kulhwch and Olwen* (*Mabinogion*). In this latter, a curious band of followers associate themselves with the king, parallels for whom are found in widely distributed *märchen*. Again, in the poetical collection, known as the *Book of Taliessin*, Arthur undertakes an expedition to the realm of darkness, and robs the king of Hades of his magic cauldron. Such were the more prominent elements, rejected by Geoffrey and those writers of the twelfth century, who combined with him to build up the cycle in its modern form.

The part, played by the *Historia Regum Britanniæ* (*c.* 1139–1148) of Geoffrey of Monmouth in the development of the Arthurian legend, has received full recognition from a succession of scholars. Representing as it does the first attempt to set forth a coherent account of Arthur's career on lines followed by later writers, Geoffrey's book marks a fresh beginning in the evolution of the legend. But it was a beginning only. The poignant stories of Lancelot and Tristram found no place in the book, nor was any recognition as yet accorded to the mystical aspect of the Arthurian theme, represented by the Holy Grail. The problem as to Geoffrey's relationship to the mass of Celtic tradition, stretching behind him, has never been completely solved, though he himself tells us that he made use of an ancient book in the British language, presented to him by Walter, Archdeacon of Oxford. This book has been assumed to be either a Welsh or a Breton MS., though a recent theory of Dr. Sebastian Evans suggests that it may have been English. There are, again, those who deny the existence of the book altogether. It is certain that nothing has yet been discovered outside of Nennius, Bede, and a few other writers, which can be regarded as in the nature of a source-book for Geoffrey's materials, though it seems impossible to doubt that he drew upon floating Celtic traditions, while indulging freely in " romancing " on his own account. The contemporary purpose of the *Historia Regum*

Britanniæ seems to have been to provide an epic, which might serve, by its joint appeal, to unite Normans and Englishmen, Welshmen and Bretons in the one common purpose of maintaining and extending the empire of the Angevins.

In, or about, 1155, Geoffrey's book was translated into Anglo-Norman verse by Wace, who added details regarding the foundation of the Round Table and other matters. Wace shows some independence, in omitting portions of Geoffrey's material, and his work is meritorious.   He links Geoffrey to Layamon.

The activities of French and Anglo-Norman writers of the twelfth century extended the range of Arthurian themes far beyond the limits imposed by Geoffrey. Once again, the Celtic problem forces itself to the front, since the possibility of Breton influence must now be reckoned with.   Intangible though the *lai*, as a literary product, may be, its influence is attested by the work of Marie de France, with its peculiar atmosphere of charm and mystery.   Except in *Lanval*, Marie's poems are not definitely associated with Arthur, and there is no proof of the existence of an elaborated Breton cycle.   But motives in the unattached *lais* can be paralleled in the Arthurian poems (cf. the *enfances* in *Tyolet* with Chrétien's *Conte del Graal*), and there is direct reference on Chrétien's part to, at least, one of them (*Guingamor*).   The personality of Kyot, cited by Wolfram von Eschenbach as his authority, is still a mystery ; though there is a possibility that Thomas' Bréri was the Bledhericus, described by Giraldus Cambrensis as a Welsh *fabulator*. The special atmosphere of the Tristram story calls for explanation, and is accounted for by nothing in the known work of Geoffrey, or of Chrétien.   Such are the general arguments put forth by the upholders of the Celtic theory.

The possibility of Celtic influence being granted, it still remains true that the organisation and extension of Arthurian romance during the twelfth century was the work of French and Norman writers. In their wake followed the German school, including some illustrious names, and, more tardily, the English. Of French writers the most distinguished was Chrétien de Troyes, who wrote, between 1150 and 1188, a *Tristan* (lost), followed by *Erec*, *Cligès*, the *Chevalier à la Charrette*, *Yvain*, and the *Conte del Graal*. The unfortunate disappearance of *Tristan* makes it impossible to compare Chrétien's treatment with those of his contemporaries, Béroul and Thomas. It may, however, be conjectured that Chrétien would have shown none of the penetrating insight into passion, characteristic of Thomas' work. *Erec* is the story of the estrangement and reconciliation of two lovers, paralleled in the *Mabinogion* by *Geraint the son of Erbin*, and familiar in Tennyson's modern version. It definitely marks the appearance of a new psychological poet. The *Chevalier à la charrette* is interesting from the fact that there Lancelot assumed a prominent *rôle*, for the first time. He is definitely the Queen's lover, and, though this appears to have been originally Gawain's part, the first form of the Lancelot-Guinevere story, as we know it, must be laid to Chrétien's credit. It is possible, judging from the evidence in Ulrich von Zatzikhoven (*c.* 1195), that the outlines of the story had been traced in an earlier French version, but this is non-extant. Nor are the Celtic *lais* extant, for which evidence has been found in the composite character of the German poem. *Yvain* is generally regarded as the best of Chrétien's romances. Having achieved the adventure of the Fountain perilous, Yvain married the lady, Laudine. Arthur and his knights were entertained at his castle, after which Yvain returned for a time to court. He overstayed his leave, and, prostrate with grief, went mad in the forest. There he associated himself with a lion, and was, henceforth, known as the Knight of the Lion. After various adventures, he was restored to his lady's affections. The *Lady of the Fountain* in the *Mabinogion* supplies a parallel

to *Yvain*, and both have been traced to a hypothetical
Anglo-Norman romance, based on a Celtic source, similar
to the tale of the *Slothful Gillie* (cf. O'Grady's *Silva
Gadelica*). The French poem supplied the materials for
Hartmann von Aue's *Iwein* (c. 1200) and for the M. E.
Ywain and Gawain (1300–1350). Chrétien's last poem, the
Conte del Graal, introduces the sacred vessel, and must be
reserved for another section.

Chrétien ranks in mediæval French literature as the
great practitioner of the courtly epic. The position
accorded in his romances to love, and the ingenuity, with
which he handles the problems arising therefrom, constitute him the founder of the psychological novel. Yet
he has no sense of passion, no mystery, and is worlds
removed from the genuine Celtic atmosphere. He is the
representative of cultured speech, the courtly poet, *par
excellence*. In intimate knowledge of the human heart
Chrétien was surpassed by his contemporary, Thomas :
the German school supplied his limitations in other
directions. Of this school, Wolfram von Eschenbach
(c. 1170–1220) stands out as the great representative of
spiritual mysticism, and Gottfried von Strassburg, whose
Tristram was composed c. 1210, as the poet of the love-
passion.

The main body of the Arthurian story, as developed by
Geoffrey and his successors of the French and German
schools, was further strengthened, towards the end of
the twelfth and the beginning of the thirteenth century,
by a series of prose romances,—the *Lancelot*, the *Mort
Artu*, the *Merlin*, based on Robert of Boron, and the
Tristan. The fusion of the knightly epic with the mystic
material of the Grail had already begun in Chrétien's
Conte del Graal. By the thirteenth century, the welding
of the two strands was finally completed in the prose of
the *Grand St. Graal* and its congeners.

The origin and meaning of the Holy Grail legends
constitute a problem as obscure as any that confronts
the student of Arthurian matters. Already in Chrétien's

Conte del Graal and its continuations the questing knight makes an appearance, represented at one stage by Perceval, at another by Gawain. Perceval failed at the outset to put the necessary question, but redeemed his fault by his subsequent conduct in avenging the murder of the Fisher-king's brother. In Wolfram von Eschenbach's *Parzival* the purely spiritual aspect of the Grail becomes prominent, and the vengeance element disappears : the M.E. *Sir Percyvelle* (1350–1400) contains neither Fisher-king nor talisman. Chrétien identifies the Grail with Joseph's vessel, but a more elaborate account of the ecclesiastical origin may be found in the *Grand St. Graal* and in Robert of Boron's *Joseph of Arimathea* (*c.* 1180). In the *Quête del St. Graal* we return to the knightly adventures, the chief figure being Galahad, Lancelot's son. Perceval is, once again, the hero of the *Didot Perceval* and the *Perlesvaus*.

A purely ecclesiastical origin has been claimed for the Grail legends by one school of critics, who discover therein a conversion of Britain legend and an attempt to set up a claim for a knightly priesthood. This view explains the prominence accorded in the cycle to Joseph of Arimathea, who is first connected with Glastonbury in an interpolation to William of Malmesbury's *De antiquitate Glastoniensis ecclesiæ*. A second school discovers the ultimate origin of the Grail material in the background of Celtic heathendom. In this connection, it is curious to observe how often the Grail is referred to in terms most readily explicable on some such assumption. Thus, it is described as a food-providing object, or again as a " stone," endowed with life-giving properties. A highly interesting theory, put forth by Miss Weston, finds the origin of the Grail ceremonial in a primitive initiation-ritual. Upon this the Christian element was imposed at a later date, but, in such a way, that the cruder elements may still be detected below the surface.

The English contribution towards the development of the cycle remains to be indicated. Follwoing upon

Geoffrey of Monmouth, the prime mover in the organisation of the material, a large number of romances appeared,
based either upon Geoffrey himself or upon other sources.
At the beginning of the thirteenth century, the story of
Arthur's career was retold by Layamon in his *Brut*,
with interesting additions concerning the elves, who
appeared at his birth, the organisation of the Round
Table, and other matters. The verse *Arthur* amounts to
no more than a bald and incoherent summary of Geoffrey.
The so-called early history is smoothly recounted in the
couplets of *Arthour and Merlin*, while the stanzaic *Le
Morte Arthur*, based on the Vulgate *Mort Artu*, concerns
itself chiefly with the loves of Lancelot and Guinevere.
In this story, the ill-starred Maid of Ascolot constitutes
a pathetic figure :

> He nolde her nought, we mow well see ;
> Forthy, deed is that white as swan ;
> This letter thereof warrant wol be,
> She plaineth on Lancelot to each man.

As for the attached knights, their histories were told,
with varying degrees of success, in *Sir Tristrem*, un-
justifiably assigned to Thomas of Erceldoun, *Ywain and
Gawain*, *Sir Percyvelle of Galles*, and the fifteenth-century
Lancelot of the Laik. Of these, *Ywain and Gawain* alone
has any distinction. As already indicated, it derives
from Chrétien, whose *Chevalier au Lion* supplied the
material for the fluent paraphrase. A noteworthy
romance, *Libeaus Desconus*, tells the story of Gawain's
son, Guinglain,—his exploit in the Vale perilous, the
winning of the sparrow-hawk, his sojourn in the *Yle d'or*,
and his final triumph in the disenchantment of his lady
by means of the *fier baiser*. The same story, with variations, appears in *Le Bel Inconnu*, the Italian *Carduino*,
and the Middle High German *Wigalois*. Apart from the
distinguished group of alliterative romances, in which
Gawain plays so prominent a part, we may regard the
Brut, Arthour and Merlin, Le Morte Arthur, Ywain and

Gawain and *Libeaus Desconus* as the most noteworthy contributions made by the older English poets to this department of romance. In the fifteenth century, Malory summed up the main features of Arthurian romance in the matchless prose of his *Morte d'Arthur*, to which his editor, Caxton, contributed a noteworthy preface :

Herein may be seen noble chyvalrye, curtosye, humanyte, frendlynesse, hardynesse, love, frendshyp, cowardyse, murdre, hate, vertue and synne. Doo after the good and leve the evyl and it shal brynge you to good fame and renommee.

(c) THE MATTER OF ANTIQUITY.

A somewhat free interpretation of Bodel's *matière de Rome* enables us to include thereunder all the romance-material derived from antiquity,—the stories of Troy, of Thebes, and of Alexander. Of these, the theme of Troy, in particular, proved attractive to a succession of men-of-letters, represented by Benoît de St. More, Guido delle Colonne, Boccaccio, Chaucer, and Shakespeare.

During the Middle Ages Homer, known only in Thebanus' *Epitome*, was largely discredited. But the story of Troy was popularised by two mediævalists, Dares and Dictys, whose names are probably forgeries. Their versions have come down to us in Latin, though Dictys, at least, appears to derive from a Greek source. The dates are quite uncertain, but Dictys has been assigned, hypothetically, to the fourth, and Dares to the sixth century A.D. Dictys Cretensis, assumed to be a follower of Idomeneus, represented the side of the Greeks, Dares Phrygius, identified with the priest of Hephæstus mentioned in the Iliad, that of the Trojans. Both accounts are brief, though Dictys is about twice as long as Dares : they represent early examples of literary forgery, both writers claiming to have been eye-witnesses of the events described. Of the two, Dares was the favourite author in the Middle Ages on account of his defence of Troy, from which almost all the nations of Western Europe assumed descent. Dares' book, accordingly, represented the starting-point of the mediæval legend of Troy. Its graphic details assured for it a large amount of credibility, while the absence of the miraculous element was in its favour. For the later development of the story, the important contributions made by Dares were the prominence accorded to Troilus, raised to the position of Trojan hero after the fall of Hector, and the concise portrait of Briseida, who thus lay to hand as a possible future heroine :

> Briseidam formosam, alta statura, candidam, capillo flavo et molli, superciliis junctis, oculis venustis, corpore æquali, blandem, affabilem, verecundam, animo simplici, piam.

About 1165, Benoît de St. More expanded Dares into a *Roman de Troie* of some 30,000 lines, drawing, at the same time, upon Dictys. Benoît's chief feat was to assign Briseida, who, under the name of Briseis, had been Achilles' mistress in Homer, to Troilus. She became the daughter of Calchas, the treacherous priest who left Troy to join the Greeks. Briseida and Troilus had already plighted troth, when she made Diomed's acquaintance in the Greek camp. The character of Briseida is only partially developed in this version, while Troilus is almost a shadow. But many elements conduced to its popularity. Though the old mythology found no place in Benoît, there was much fairy-lore. In fact, the classical story was completely mediævalised, and re-told with vigour.

In the same century, about 1187, Joseph of Exeter wrote a Latin poem, *De Bello Trojano*, in which he drew upon Dares, Benoît, Statius, and Ovid. But the importance of Joseph of Exeter rests upon his form, rather than his material. The book was formerly attributed to Cornelius Nepos.

Towards the end of the thirteenth century, Benoît's poem was plagiarised by Guido delle Colonne, a Sicilian, whose *Historia Trojana* became enormously popular.

Until recently, the credit due to Benoît was accorded entirely to Guido, though his book was practically a translation of his predecessor's work into Latin prose, with additions from Virgil and Ovid. The next important name is Boccaccio, who, in his *Filostrato* (1344–1350), centred his attention on the early relationships between Troilus and the lady, whom he re-names Griseida. She is introduced as a widow, with Pandaro in the *rôle* of intermediary. The conception of Troilus constitutes the outstanding feature of Boccaccio's treatment.

The English had been familiar with the general story of Troy since the time of Geoffrey of Monmouth, to whom Chaucer afterwards accorded a distinguished place among the historians. Before 1400, two versions of the romantic history appeared in English, the *Gest Historiale of the Destruction of Troy* (1350–1400) and the *Seege of Troye* (1350–1400). Of these, the former was a close imitation, in alliterative verse, of Guido, the latter a free version, based on Benoît. The *Gest Historiale* has been assigned, without satisfactory evidence, to Huchoun. It provides a vigorous example of the alliterative style of the fourteenth century. In the prologue, the author reviews the history of the romance, and concludes with an apt tribute to Guido :

In this shall faithfully be founden to the fer ende,
All þe dedis bydene as þai done were ;
How þe groundes first grew, and þe grete hate,
Bothe of torfer and tene þat hom tide aftur.
And here fynde shall ye faire of þe felle peopull,
What kynges þere come of costes aboute :
Of dukes full doughty, and of derffe erles,
That assembled to þe citie þat sawte to defend :
Of the Grekys þat were gedret how gret was þe nowmber,
How mony knightes þere come and kynges enarmede,
And what dukes thedur droghe for dedis of were :
What shippes þere were shene, and shalkes within,
Bothe of barges and buernes þat broght were fro Grese :

And all the batels on bent þe buernes betwene.
What duke þat was dede through dyntes of hond,
Who fallen was in ffylde, and how it fore after :
Bothe of truse and of trayne þe truthe shalt þu here,
And all the ferlies þat fell unto the ferre ende.

About the same time, a worthier poet turned to Boccaccio's version, and evolved therefrom an independent
masterpiece, *Troilus and Criseyde.* Chaucer devoted
himself mainly to the character of Pandarus, and, in so
doing, produced the first great psychological poem in
English. At the beginning of the fifteenth century, a
capable version of Guido appeared from the pen of
Lydgate, and to the same century are assigned certain
Scottish fragments of the Troy story. Caxton's famous
Recueyll of the historyes of Troye (*c.* 1474) represents a
translation from the French of Raoul le Fevre. But the
most original contribution made during this century was
Henryson's *Testament of Cresseid*, in which the poet brings
down vengeance upon the lady's head. The English
versions culminate in Shakespeare's *Troilus and Cressida*,
a play which has given rise to many problems, and in
which the great dramatist saw fit to adopt a debased
view of the characters, generally.

The nucleus of the romantic history of Alexander, as
known to Western Europe, appears to have been formed
early in the Christian era in the so-called *Pseudo-Callis-
thenes.* This latter, which belongs to the same category
as the *Turpin* and *Dares*, affords another example of
mediæval literary forgery : certain features of the book
point, indeed, to an Egyptian origin. By the end of
the twelfth century, various Latin versions had appeared,
the earliest by Julius Valerius (*c.* 340) : an epitome of
this appeared in the ninth century. More important
was the *Historia Alexandri Magni de Proeliis*, composed
in the tenth century by the Archpriest Leo, after a visit
to Constantinople. More or less independent were the
Epistola Alexandri ad Aristotelem, the *Iter ad Paradisum*,

and the Latin correspondence between Alexander and Dindimus.

Towards the end of the eleventh century, the Alexander story was retold in French by Alberic de Briançon, to be followed in the next century by the decasyllabic *Roman d'Alixandre* of Lambert le Tort and Alexandre de Bernai. In contrast to that of Alberic, this latter version abounded in the marvels of the East and became instantly popular. To the end of the twelfth century is assigned the *Vengeance Alexandre* of Gui de Cambrai : the thirteenth century claims the Anglo-Norman *Roman de toute chevalerie* of Eustache of Kent, the source of the M.E. *King Alisaunder*. Jacques de Longuyon's *Vœux du paon* (c. 1312) introduced a new episode, afterwards handled by the author of the Scottish *Buik of Alexander* (fifteenth century) and by Sir Gilbert Hay. The theme of "the Nine Worthies" was treated at length, for the first time, by Longuyon, and imitated, for example, in the fourteenth century *Parlement of the Three Ages*.

During the Anglo-Saxon period, the *Epistola Alexandri ad Aristotelem* and the *De rebus in Oriente mirabilibus* were translated into English, to be followed, after the Conquest, by a remarkable series of books, of which the pioneer was the metrical *King Alisaunder* (c. 1330). After a prologue of forty lines, in four-beat metre, which promises matter "delicious to listen to," the author introduces the wizard, Neptanabus (the Nakhtenephen of ancient Egypt), attempting to discover, by sortilege, the prospects of the Persian invasion. Then follows an account of the wizard's relations with Phillip's queen, leading up to the mysterious birth of Alexander. The boy soon displayed his dexterity by taming Bulsifal (Bucephalus), and, afterwards, effectively avenging his parents upon Neptanabus. During a military expedition against Carthage, Alexander learnt of his mother's relations with Pausanias, and, returning, slew her paramour. Having succeeded to his father's dominions, Alexander inaugurated his career of conquest by an

expedition against Thrace and Italy. At Tripoli, he saw
the image of Neptanabus, and, definitely, learnt his
parentage, for the first time. During the siege of Tyre,
he was insulted by the inhabitants, and, shortly- afterwards, Darius sent him a number of childish presents,—
a top, a scourge, and a purse. The completion of the
war with Darius was delayed by a progress through Greece,
during which Alexander conquered Thebes and received
the submission of Athens, but, returning to the East,
he, finally, defeated Darius. So ends the first part.

In the second, Porus takes the place of Darius. The
interest turns upon the wonders of the East, the fauna
and flora, as well as the peoples, described being closely
akin to those in Sir John Mandeville :

> Another folk there is biside ;
> Houndynges men clepeth hem wide.
> From the brèst to the grounde
> Men hy ben, abouen houndes.
> Berkyng of houndes hy habbe.
> Her honden, withouten gabbe,
> Ben yshuldred as an fysshe,
> And clawed after hound, iwisse (ll. 4962–69).

During an interval of peace, Alexander journeyed with
Porus to the world's end, where he saw two golden images,
identified with the pillars of Hercules. The terrestrial
paradise is alluded to, but briefly. The sole love-element
is provided by the Queen Candace episode, which occupies
considerable space. With much detail, the author describes the trees of the sun and moon, and from these
Alexander learnt the exact nature of his death :

> Forth Alisaundre gan wende,
> Til he come to theo trowes ende.
> Notemugge, and the sedewale,
> On heom smullith, and the wodewale,
> Theo canel and the licoris,
> And swete savour ymeynt, ywis (ll. 6790–95).

After the founding of Alexandria, the campaign against

Porus was brought to a successful termination, the romance concluding with an account of Antipater's treachery and the death of Alexander.

The above summary will serve to indicate the main lines of the romantic history of Alexander. In the M.E. version, many elements are omitted, in particular the " Foray of Gaza," though this does not appear to have been one of the primary elements, and the Fountain of Youth : but the early history is recorded with some completeness. *King Alisaunder* bears all the marks of a popular poem, but it is by no means lacking in charm. The style is vigorous and reminiscent of the older epic. Short reflective and didactic passages, enlarging upon the brevity of life, the futility of battle, the ill-effects of sin, the attractions of the hall, and the characteristics of women, enhance the charm of the narrative. The pithy proverb finds an entrance, here and there, while the tendency to moralise, is so characteristic of the poet that he concludes on this note. Most attractive of all are the so-called " lyrical intermezzos," with which each section is introduced, little nature-passages of a quality altogether charming :

> In tyme of heruest mery it is ynough ;
> Peres and apples hongeth on bough.
> The hayward bloweth mery his horne ;
> In eueryche felde ripe is corne ;
> The grapes hongen on the vyne :
> Swete is trewe loue and fyne (ll. 5754–59).

In the fourteenth century, under the influence of new literary influences, the story of Alexander was re-told, in alliterative verse, in three independent poems, known respectively as *Alisaunder*, *Alexander and Dindimus*, and the *Wars of Alexander*. Taken together, these pieces provide a complete view of Alexander's career, including his correspondence with the king of the Brahmans. At the same time there is considerable over-lapping. The main source, was, undoubtedly, Leo's *De Proeliis*, but

the Dindimus material, in particular, must be accounted
for otherwise. The poems provide accomplished examples
of the alliterative manner, and the learned allusions
contrast with the *naïve* matter of the metrical romances.
Contrast the following description of the portents at
Alexander's birth with the corresponding passage in
King Alisaunder :

þe liȝt lemand late   ·   laschis fra þe heuyn,
Thonere thrastis ware thra   ·   thristid þe welkyn,
Cloudis clenely to-clefe   ·   clatird unfaire,
All blakenid aboute   ·   and boris þe son.
Wild wedirs up werpe   ·   and þe wynd ryse,
And all flames þe flode   ·   as it fire were,
Nowe briȝt, nowe blaa   ·   nowe on blase efter,
And þan ouer-qwelmys in a qwirre   ·   and qwatis euer e -like.
þan slike a derknes þar. drafe   ·   and demyd þe skewys,
As blesenand as bale fyre   ·   and blake as þe hell
þat it was neuer bot as nyȝt   ·   fra þe none tyme
Till it to mydday was meten   ·   on þe morne efter.
                    (*Wars of Alexander*, ll. 553–64.)

The tendency towards didacticism is characteristic of
the alliterative school, in general, and the correspondence
between Alexander and Dindimus may be regarded as
an academic discussion on the respective claims of the
active and the contemplative life.   One singularly happy
passage, describing the attractions of the woods fre-
quented by the Gymnosophists, serves to illustrate the
close relationship to the Latin sources.   Compare *Alexander and Dindimus* ll. 494–503 with the following from
the anonymous *De Bragmanis* :

Delectamur   etiam   videre   florigeros   campos   ex   quibus
in nostros nares suavissimus odor intrat.   Delectamur etiam
in optimis locis siluarum et fontium in quibus iocundissimas
avium audimus cantilenas.

The prose epitome of the *Life of Alexander* in the
Dublin MS. represents an attempt to arrive at a true
historic estimate, but the Thornton *Life* (fifteenth

century) abounds in the usual fabulous material. The Scottish *Buik of Alexander* (fifteenth century) is episodic, treating of the Foray of Gadderis, the Avows of Alexander, and the Great Battle of Effesoun in a metre strongly reminiscent of Barbour. Sir Gilbert Hay's long poem recounts the whole history once again.

Apart from Chaucer's *Knight's Tale*, no M.E. version of the story of Thebes appeared before the end of the fourteenth century. Chaucer's story dealt merely with an episode, on the lines of Boccaccio's *Teseide*, but Lydgate was to provide a fuller survey of the subject. During the Elizabethan period, the Chaucerian episode was selected for dramatic treatment by a number of writers, including Richard Edwards and, possibly, Shakespeare himself.

XIII. THE SHORT STORY

The mediæval short story, whether in the form of *conte dévot, exemplum, fable*, or *fabliau*, was everywhere a highly popular type. The art of story-telling is limited to no particular age, or people, and variations of particular stories may spring up simultaneously in different areas. But, occasionally, we come upon traces of actual borrowing, of the direct influence of one literature upon another. This appears to be the case with the mediæval beast-fable, in particular.

The history of the Æsopian fable, as worked out by Jacobs, carries us back to the Buddhist Birth-stories in the *Jātakas* of the fifth century B.C., behind which existed an undetermined background of fable, with the Indian sage, Kasyapa, as the central figure. Assuming the identification of Kasyapa with the Lybian Kybises, of

whom Babrius speaks, we at once discover a link between
Oriental and Roman literature. Babrius' reference to
Æsop further associates the Roman with the Greek fable,
through Demetrius Phalereus, who compiled c. 300 B.C.
a Λόγων Αἰσωπείων συναγωγαί. The intermediary between
Babrius and his predecessors was a certain Nicostratus,
who, in the reign of Marcus Aurelius, combined Demetrius and Kybises. In the fourth century, the work of
Babrius was continued by Avian. Meantime, in the
first century A.D., a Greek freedman, Phaedrus, had
turned Demetrius into Latin iambics. During the
Middle Ages, Phaedrus masqueraded under the names
of *Romulus, Rufus*, and *Ademar*, and exerted a powerful
influence on the history of the fable in the West.

During the twelfth century, England became the home
of the Æsopic fable. The tenth-century *Romulus* was
done into Latin verse by a certain Gualterus Anglicus,
from whom derive versions in French and Italian. Alexander Neckam, by essaying the same task, became responsible for further versions in French. A curious interest
attaches to the obscure Alfred of England, whom Marie de
France signalised as an enthusiast for Æsop, and employed
as her source :

> Li reis Alvrez qui mult l'ama
> Le translata puis en engleis
> E jo l'ai rimé en franceis.

The Eastern element in Marie has prompted the theory that
this Alfred, confused by her with the Saxon king, had
translated the Arabic Æsop into Latin in the twelfth
century, with the assistance of a Jewish collaborator.
In this way, through the intermediary of the East, the
influence of Babrius passed to England. In the fifteenth
century, Caxton translated his famous *Esope* from the
French of Machault, based, in its turn, on the *Äsop* of
Steinhöwel (c. 1480). Steinhöwel's book was woven
from many sources, *Romulus*, Avian, Greek prose versions,
and portions of the twelfth-century Alfred. We are,

thus, carried back in one direction to Phaedrus, in another to Babrius, and, ultimately to the Greek and Oriental sources of the beast-fable. From the twelfth to the fourteenth century, the history of the French and Latin fable in England is represented by names like Marie de France, Gualterus Anglicus, Alexander Neckam, Odo of Cheriton, and John of Sheppey: the native fable, on the other hand, survives in mere fragments, embedded in the *Owl and the Nightingale*, *Barlaam and Josaphat*, the *Ayenbite of Inwyt*, *Piers Plowman*, Barbour, Gower, and Chaucer. That the type had long been popular in England is proved by the illustrations on the Bayeux tapestry. More significant is the evidence of the English tags in Odo of Cheriton and Nicole de Bozon, pointing to the existence of a large fable-literature, which has not survived.

The beast-epic was a characteristic creation of the Middle Ages, a composite of many parts. The nucleus is, perhaps, to be found in the *Ecbasis captivi*, a Latin hexameter poem composed by a German monk *c.* 940, which relates, with allegorical intent, the escape of a calf from the clutches of a wolf. A second Latin work, the *Ysengrimus* of Nivard (twelfth century), was influential in promoting the formation of the French *Roman de Renart*, with its various "branches." Heinrich der Glichzare's poem (*c.* 1180), based in its turn upon the French, relates how the fox cured the lion's ear and afterwards poisoned his master. Caxton's version was derived, ultimately, from the Flemish *Roman van den Vos Reinarde* of the thirteenth century, through the intermediary of German.

Early in the thirteenth century, the *dramatis personæ* of the beast-epic were familiar in England, judging from names like Isengrim, Reynard, and Teburgus in Odo of Cheriton's collection, and, before the end of the century, England had made her chief contribution to the epic in the humorous *Vox and the Wolf*. Here, the wit is equal to the French, and, though the author probably found his model in one of the branches of the *Roman de Renart*, he abounds in originality and humour. The opening dialogue between the cock and the fox is the best thing in its way before the *Nun Priest's Tale*, the confession of the wolf before his descent into " Paradise " is, at least, equal to that in the *Roman*, while the passage, in which the wolf is mistaken for the Devil, forms an apt termination. The lack of parallels for the story, as a whole, suggests popular derivation.

Another type of short story, the *exemplum*, was used by religious writers for illustrative purposes. Primitive examples occur in Oriental literature, in the *Jātakas*, the *Fables of Bidpai*, and *Barlaam and Josaphat*, the subjects being frequently chosen from the animal world. In this way, the *exemplum* came to include the beast-fable, which it employed with didactic purpose.

The West provided countless examples of this type of short story, collected into special hand-books, or embedded in sermon-literature. Already in the first century, Valerius Maximus had compiled a series of anecdotes, *De factis dictisque memorabilibus*, which ranks as a pioneer book of its kind. More important was the *Disciplina clericalis* of Petrus Alphonsus (twelfth century), the first Western collection of Eastern tales. This book, with its variety of short and long anecdotes, became highly popular, and at least sixty MSS. are extant. Its influence was wide-spread in both the collections and sermon-books ; the *Gesta Romanorum*, Jacques de Vitry, Albertano da Brescia, Thomas of Cantimpré, the *Alphabetum Narrationum*, and Bromyard's *Summa predicantium* being among its debtors. Under the title of *Fables of Alfonce*, the collection appeared as an appendage to Caxton's translation of Æsop. The stories themselves became familiar to practitioners of literature ; for example, that of the woman, who, after being immured by a jealous husband, escaped by throwing a stone into a well was adopted by Boccaccio and Molière, among others. In English, the earliest examples were the so-called *bīsna* of Ælfred's translations, which reappeared in the *Blickling Homilies*, in Ælfric, and Wulfstan. After the Conquest, reforms introduced into the art of preaching by the friars resulted in an increased use of *exempla* in the pulpit. They figure, also, in homiletic works like the *Ancren Riwle*, the *Ayenbite of Inwyt, Handlyng Synne*, in the *Saints' Lives*, in books of instruction and entertainment, like John of Salisbury's *Polycraticus*, Map's *De nugis curialium*, Neckam's *De naturis rerum*, and occur scattered throughout the works of Gower and Chaucer.

The short story in verse, known as the *fabliau*, derived its inspiration from ordinary life. Originating in the oral tradition of East and West, these stories assumed, in the first instance, a definitely French spirit and a form, the basis of which was the eight-syllabled line. The majority were anonymous, though a number have been associated with the names of Rutebeuf, Henri d'Andeli, Huon le Roi, etc. The point of view is highly humorous : they abound in themes more, or less, gross, in genial satire levelled against women and priests, in malicious turns, and a licence, not exclusively *bourgeois*. In general, they represent a reaction against the dominance of the courtly romance, though interest in them was not confined to a particular social class. The hostility of responsible Englishmen, exemplified by references to " tales untoun," and the general strictures of writers like Chaucer and Langland reduced the number of English survivals. Sufficient remain, however, to attest the popularity of the type in England. In the Auchinleck MS. (1330–1340), for example, we come upon a story entitled the *Peniworth of Witte*, of which the fifteenth-century version is renamed *How a Merchande dyd hys wyfe betray*. This piece has a utilitarian intent, showing how the treacherous husband ultimately proved his wife's loyalty superior to that of his leman. A curious interest attaches to *Dame Sirith* (*c.* 1260), the outstanding example of its type in English. Originally, it derived from the far East, and is paralleled in Sanskrit and Arabic versions. There is evidence that the tale was widely used as an *exemplum*, hence its appearance in collections like the *Disciplina clericalis*. In some ways, *Dame Sirith* is superior to the general type of *fabliau*, and, in its conception of the procuress, leans towards comedy : in fact, the curious little interlude, *De clerico et puella*, well illustrates the dramatic possibilities of the story. The *motif* whereby the lady is induced to yield, through fear of being transformed into a bitch, is Eastern, but the theme is worked out dramatically by an abundant use of dialogue. Another example, illustrating the mixture of types, is *Sir Cleges*, in which the nucleus of a *fabliau* has been associated with a pious tale and a background of Arthurian romance. This relates the old-time story of the reward accorded to the covetous man, Sir Cleges sharing his gifts in advance, and choosing twelve blows to be distributed, where he pleases. Associated with this is the miracle of the cherries, sent to the pious knight in answer to prayer. Fortunately, the more spirited part is that dealing with the apt distribution of the gifts :

> To the porter com he yare ;
> ffoure strokes payd he thare ;
> His parte had he tho.
> Aftyr-werd many a dey
> He wold wern no man the wey,
> Nether to ryde ne go.
> The fyrst stroke he leyd hym onne,
> He brake atwo hys schulder bone
> And hys ryght arme also.

Later, in the fifteenth century, the list of *fabliaus* was swelled by such pieces as the *Wright's Chaste Wife*, the *Tale of the basin*, the *Friar and the boy*, the *Tournament of Totenham*, and *How a sergeant would learn to be a friar*.

The suspicion with which fiction was regarded in pre-Conquest times is apparent from Ælfred's attitude towards the Greek fable. Yet there are numerous examples of the *conte dévot* or religious story in Old English from Bede to Ælfric. Again, the West-Saxon translation of Gregory's *Dialogues*, compiled in rivalry with the *Vitæ Patrum* (fifth century), had introduced crude legends of the saints, such as how Frigidianus diverted the course of the Serchio with a rake. A characteristic feature of the thirteenth century was the cult of the Virgin, and in France collections of *Miracles* were compiled by Gautier de Coinci and others. In English, there survive, besides a number of detached miracles, the Harley series (seven), the Phillipps (eighteen), and the Vernon (nine), of which latter the story of the child slain by the Jews is well known for its connection with the *Prioress's Tale*. Another tells how a merchant, having pledged the Virgin as his surety for a sum of money, bethought himself of the payment at the last moment. Placing the money in a chest, he cast it into the sea, whence, by the intervention of the Virgin, it arrived at its destination. The Jew afterwards denied having received the money, but was convicted by the Virgin.

Despite the crudities of many of these stories, they are related with earnestness, and it is regrettable that so many have perished. Of religious stories, unconnected with the Virgin cult, there are a fair number. The *Gast of Gy*, a sophisticated piece from the hands of the clerics, is too obviously propagandist, while the *Trentalle Sancti Gregorii* has little interest, apart from its connection with the alliterative *Awntyrs off Arthure*. The moral of the *Eremyte and the Outlawe* is dubious, though its kinship with the French *Du chevalier au barisel* makes it worthy of attention. After these, it is a relief to turn to the comic narratives of the *Narratio Sancti Augustini* and the *Smith and his dame*. In the former, the Devil is observed to note down the conversation of three women in church, the deduction being that it is imprudent to talk during the celebration of the mass. The smith, in his efforts to forge a beautiful wife in imitation of our

Lord, thrusts her into the fire, whence she is rescued only by divine intervention.

Reference has already been made to the collections of *exempla*. It remains to mention, as a work of a more general character, the *Seven Sages of Rome*. The scheme is similar to that of the *Decameron* and of the *Canterbury Tales*, while the framework and many of the stories derive from the *Book of Sindibad*. A young prince, wrongfully accused by his stepmother, is defended by seven sages, who relate stories, in turn, over a period of seven days. The queen replies to each, but the tables are finally turned by the prince's own narration. Many of the stories, such as that of the faithful hound slain by his master, are of world-wide distribution.

XIV.   DIDACTIC LITERATURE

The didactic literature of the Middle English period includes among its dominant types the proverb, the dialogue, and the scientific treatise. In almost every respect, it represents a continuation of the tradition, inaugurated during the earlier period.

Apart from the literary monuments, the Middle English proverb found a home in such collections as those ascribed to Alfred and Hendyng. Others appeared anonymously in MSS. Trinity (thirteenth century) and Douce (fifteenth century) and the *Wise Man's Proverbs* of MS. Bodley 9. In some cases, these have special interest owing to their bi-lingual character.

The *Proverbs of Alfred* so-called date from about the middle of the twelfth century, and display curious links with the stressed alliterative verse of Old English :

þùs qúeþ Álurèd
þe eórl aǹd þe éþelỳng
ibúreþ uǹder gódne kìng.
þàt lónd to lédèn
myd láwelỳche dédèn (Jesus Coll. MS.).

The background is provided by an assembly at Seaford, where the king dispenses wisdom to his bishops, thanes, and earls : the Trinity version, however, confuses the original scheme towards the close, by addressing its admonition to a son, in particular. The proverbs group themselves round the king, the knight, and the average man, counselling piety, justice, diligence, and humility. Domestic relations are treated at some length. A curious piece of superstition as to the danger of associating with a red-haired man brings the collection to a close.

The old-world material in the thirteenth century *Proverbs of Hendyng* has undergone re-arrangement on the French model, since, despite the alliterative phrasing and the connection with the older *Salomon and Saturn* literature, its stanzaic arrangement is novel. In every instance, the proverbs are introduced by a six-lined stanza rhymed, as a rule, aabccb. The general arrangement is unsystematic, but the matter, with its counsels regarding travel, control of children, exercise of the memory, home-keeping, borrowing and lending, possesses interest. The Germanic spirit is best exemplified in the cautions regarding lending and hasty speech : " The hasty tongue sings its own mishap,"—so runs a precept in the Icelandic *Hávamál*, paralleled in our collection by the following stanza :

> Wis man halt is wordes ynne ;
> For he nul no gle bygynne,
>   Er he have tempred is pype.
> Sot is sot, and that is sene ;
> For he wol speke wordes grene,
>   Er þen hue buen rype.
> " Sottes bolt is sone shote " ;
>   Quoþ Hendyng.

The popular mediæval school-book, the *Distichs of Cato* (fourth to fifth centuries), of which the nucleus, *Cato magnus*, must be distinguished from the supplementary *Cato parvus*, had appeared in translated form already in the Anglo-Saxon period : in Middle English, there were several versions, culminating in that of Caxton (1483). Allied to this is the little piece, *How the wyse man taught hys sone*, which warns against " newefangylnes," boisterous behaviour, and late hours, and advises caution in the choice of a wife. More interesting is the related *How the goode wif taught hir daughter*, in stanzas. The cautions against unseemly behaviour in church remind one of *A lutel soth sermun*, while the implication that young girls were accustomed to frequent wrestling and shooting-matches adds to our knowledge of the period. The inter-relationship between the collections is illustrated by such proverbs as " Leue childe lore behoveth " and " Borrowed thinge wole home," for which parallels occur in *Hendyng*.

Dialogue literature, whether purely catechetical, or under the more literary aspect of the dispute and the *débat*, has been a favourite medium of instruction in all countries. The *Psychomachia* (fourth century) of Prudentius provides an early example in the West, and to the same class belong the Northern flyting-poems. The Old English contention, the *Soul and the Body*, is actually a monologue, but debates on the same theme made an appearance soon after the Conquest. Attention has already been called to the early translation of the *Elucidarium*, the popularity of which is proved by its re-appearance, in 1508, as a chap-book, from the press of Wynkyn de Worde. The early Middle English dialogue, *Vices and Virtues* (c. 1200), is a sober little tractate, consisting of a soul's confession and Reason's reply thereto. Too much attention may be given to the observance of times and seasons : it is easy to sink " the boat of the soul." Have faith and practise the three Christian virtues. Classified by Chaucer as a romance, *Ypotis* (c. 1300) is actually a didactic poem, in which a child reasons with the Emperor Hadrian upon theology and natural history. Epictetus had figured in the Latin dialogue, *Adrian et Epictitus* : here he is identified with the child Christ, who declares at parting :

> I am he that thee wrought
> And on the rood thee dearly bought.

Pathos and dramatic force distinguish the dialogue, the *Virgin and Christ on the Cross* (c. 1310), of MS. Harley 2253 :

> " Stond wel, moder, under rode,
> Byhold þy Sone wiþ glade mode ;
> Blyþe, moder, myht þou be ! "
> " Sone, hou shulde I blyþe stonde ?
> I se þin fet, I se þin honde,
> Nayled to þe harde tre."

Interesting apocryphal material and experimentations in rhyme characterise the minor disputations, the *Childe Jesu and maistres of the lawe, A cristenemon and a Jew,* and *Mary and the Cross.*

The twelfth-century outburst of poetry in Provence had produced among its varieties the *tenson* and the *partimen.* In their employment of retort and personalities, these are akin to the *Owl and the Nightingale,* but reveal none of its narrative and dramatic qualities. Closer analogues to the Middle English poem may be found among the *carmina burana* and their French imitations. The *Owl and the Nightingale* towers high above the average dialogue : it is a genuine debate, in which justice is accorded to both sides. The disputants are chosen from among the birds, a convention of the animal-fable, while another convention appears in the opening scene in the dale. But the descriptions spring from a genuine enthusiast, whose thumb-nail sketches constitute a valuable contribution to the history of English nature-poetry. The poem has the advantage

of being secular, and of bringing us close to actuality.
It is a genuine piece of literature, humorous, sympathetic,
patriotic, and sane. Metrically, its achievement is a
triumph, since, while adopting the couplet as his norm,
the poet has not submitted to its shackles. The extra-
syllable is employed freely and, as a compromise between
native and foreign practice, both end- and middle-rhyme.
Conjecture has run high as to the purpose of the poem,
whether the respective claims of love and didactic poetry,
pleasure and duty, art and philosophy, or the æsthetic
and the ascetic life. The poet's conclusion is left in
doubt, the contestants being referred to an adjudicator
who does not appear, but his ability to see both sides
of a dispute with clearness is beyond question.
Altogether, the *Owl and the Nightingale* must be regarded
as the most original poem in Middle English before
Chaucer.

Writing some fifty years later, the author of the
Thrush and the Nightingale appears to have been in-
fluenced by the general idea of his predecessor. The
nightingale carries the day against the thrush, and it
may possibly have appeared to the writer that the drift
of the argument in the older poem favoured the nightingale rather than the owl. At any rate, despite the
thrush's appeal to the stories of Alexander, Samson, and
Gawain, as illustrating feminine wiles, the debate is
settled by the reminder that Christ was born of a woman.
This little piece in twelve-lined stanzas has dramatic
qualities, though the speeches succeed one another
without transition, to the neglect of narrative. The
opening lines are reminiscent of the familiar spring-song,
" Lenten ys come with love to toune " in MS. Harl.
2253.

The scientific writings of the Middle English period
make no claim to literary quality : in any case, their
matter sets them apart as ancillary to literature rather
than actually literary. Following in the wake of Bede
and other Anglo-Latinists, tractates were composed

upon the *Seven Ages of the World* and the *Science of cirurgie.*
There was also a rhymed treatise on *Bloodletting* in
octosyllables. Less practical was the *Treatise on dreams*,
though interest in this border-line science is well attested
by contemporary literature :

> Mon that bryddes syth slepynde,
> Him is toward gret wynnynge.
> Mon that meteth of lomb ant got
> That tokneth confort, God yt wot !

The natural history of animals interested the mediæval
mind mainly in so far as it was capable of moral application. In the East Midland *Bestiary* (1200–1250), the
material of the Latin *Physiologus* is rendered in a curious
amalgam of old and new rhythms, while alliteration
figures side by side with rhyme. The manner is *naïve*
and sometimes amusing. Thirteen birds and animals
are introduced, the account of each being followed by a
" signification." Thus, the lion represents our Lord,
the eagle human nature, and the whale the devil. A
geographical poem in verse, little more than a rough list
of names, is extant in a fourteenth-century MS., and
the clerics appear to have attempted to win pilgrims
abroad by versified accounts of the *Stations of Rome*
and of *Jerusalem.* The gem of the scientific compilations
was, however, Trevisa's translation of the *De Proprie-
tatibus* of Bartholomeus Anglicus. The material ranges
from science to natural history, and includes an account
of mediæval society. Here we may read how sleep can
be produced with the rinds of mandragora, sodden in
wine ; how the peacock displays the voice of a friend,
the head of a serpent, and the gait of a thief ; how
dragons, four or five in number, fasten their tails together
and sail over the sea to get food. In the Renaissance
period, the book was to prove a mine of similes to writers
like Du Bartas, Spenser, and Jonson.

XV. LYRIC AND VERSE-SATIRE

Mediæval lyric provides an invaluable picture of prosodic development under the tutelage of Latin and Romance. Latin prosody, during the period of the decline and fall, had undergone a sea-change and emerged remodelled. The contrast between the old and the new may be exemplified by setting side by side a Horatian metre (in this case the Alcaic) with one from Ambrose :

Nūnc/ēst bĭ/bēndūm, / / nūnc pĕdĕ/lībĕ/rō
pūl/sāndă / tēllūs, / / nūnc Sălĭ/ārĭ/bŭs
ōr/nārĕ / pūlvī/nār dĕ/ōrŭm
tēmpŭs ĕ/rāt dăpĭ/būs, sŏ/dālēs.

Here the rhythm appears cabin'd, cribb'd, and confined by rules of quantity. In the Ambrosian verse, on the other hand, the rhetorical accent determines the verse-stress, and the metre is reduced to comparative simplicity :

Præco diei jam sonat
noctis profundæ pervigil,
nocturna lux viantibus
a nocte noctem segregans.

These lines from the hymn, *Æterne rerum conditor*, reveal the model of the English iambic dimeter.

Further, rhyme as an ornament of verse played a large part in Latin hymnology and goliardic poetry, and it is here and in Romance that the source of this new element is to be found, despite the fact that Old English had seen such an experiment as the *Rhyming poem*.

Mediæval lyric attained to its highest artistic develop-ment in Provence during the latter part of the twelfth and the beginning of the thirteenth century. The highly elaborate character of this poetry is illustrated by the vast variety of its experiments in stanza. The *chanson d'amour* was the most approved type, the tribute of a lover to a mistress, not always expressive of personal emotion, but often self-conscious and conventional. The *trobador* was the composer and corresponded to the Northern *trouvère*. The names of nearly five hundred of these have come down to us, the most famous being the Count of Poitou, Jaufre Rudel, Bernart de Ventadorn, Bertran de Born, and Peire Vidal. Besides the *chanson* or love-song, the chief forms were the *sirventes* or satire, the *planh* or funeral song, the *tenso* or debate, the *joc partit*, the *pastorale*, the *alba*, and the *serena*. It may be noted that the music, which was altogether as important as the words, has come down in part, as in the instance of the English *Cuckoo song*. The variety of the accompaniments naturally resulted in the introduction of new rhythms. The romantic side of troubadour life is best illustrated by the story of Rudel, who, loving the Countess of Tripoli without ever having seen her, fared abroad in quest of her, and, in the end, died in her arms. It matters little whether the story be well-founded or not : what we have is :

> " The desire of the moth for the star,
> Of the night for the morrow,
> The devotion to something afar
> From the sphere of *his* sorrow."

Dante selected three names as representative of the styles of the *trobadors*,—Bertran de Born who sang of arms, Arnaut Daniel whose theme was love, and Guiraut de Bornelh, the singer of uprightness, honour, and virtue. But Bernart de Ventadorn is the most interesting to Englishmen as the associate of Eleanor of Guienne and the poet of the clear style, *trobar clar*. The debt of Italian to the poetry of Provence was immense, and it must be reckoned with in the history of English and German poetry. The sonnet and *terza rima*, indeed, originated in Provence.

Side by side with the Provençal, lyric had appeared in Northern France, in the various forms of *chanson de toile, chanson à danser, ballette, rondet,* and *vireli,* and for these priority has even been claimed. But, from the middle of the twelfth century, the influence of the South was felt to the full in the Northern area, though the lyric continued to be handled with sufficient originality. The *romance* and the *pastourelle* were the dominant forms, composed in stanzas with refrains and more dramatic in quality than their Southern equivalents. Later, *chansons d'amour*, *jeux partis*, and *serventois* swelled the roll of lyric types. The exultant delight in mere living, characteristic of Thibaut de Champagne and of Colin Muset, serves to show what was being accomplished in the Northern French dialect during the thirteenth century :

> En mai, quant li rossignolet
> Chantent cler ou vert boissonet,
> Lors m'estuet faire un flajolet,
> Si le ferai d'un saucelet,
> Qu'il m'estuet d'amors flajoler
> Et chapelet de flor porter
> Por moi deduire et deporter,
> Qu'adès ne doit on pas muser.
>
> (Colin Muset ed. Bédier.)

The beginnings of English lyric, Anglo-Saxon experiments being excluded for formal reasons, date back, as far as is known to *Canute's Song* and the *Godric hymns*. The former, assigned to the middle of the twelfth century, is composed in alliterative lines, rhymed and assonanced : the latter, which have come down accompanied by their music, illustrate the first gropings in the direction of the regular four-beat metre. The *Hymn to the Virgin* reveals some sense of style :

> Sainte Marie, Cristes bur,
> Maidenes clenhad, moderes flur,
> Dilie mine sinne, rixe in min mod,
> Bring me to winne wið self God.

The impulse to song is natural everywhere, but we have only indirect evidence of its existence in England before the reign of Henry III ; for example, the little refrain, *Swete lemman, thin are*, cited by Giraldus Cambrensis. Under Henry II, literary relations had been established with the Continent, and England became the home of many French and Provençal poets. For a long period, English and French lyric developed side by side, as is apparent from the bi-lingual character of MS. Harleian 2253. Meantime, the University system was responsible for a school of goliardic poems, *carmina burana*, with which we must reckon, no less than with Romance, in the development of English lyric.

The parallelism between English and French stanzaic forms may be illustrated by setting side by side such a poem as the following from Bartsch's *Romanzen und Pastourellen* and No. XI in Wright's *Specimens from the Harleian MS.* :

> Main se leva bele Aeliz :
> dormez, jaloux, ge vous en pri.
> biau se para, miex se vesti,
>   desoz le raim.
> mignotement la voi venir
>   cele que j'aim.

Looking forward, we find this to be the stanza of Burns' *Scotch drink*, known in Middle English as the Octovian, from its employment in the romance so-called. The origin of the tail-rhymed stanza (whether of 6, 8, or 12 lines) is found in Latin hymnology :

> Lauda Sion salvatorem
> lauda ducem et pastorem
>   in hymnis et canticis :
> quantum potes, tantum aude
> quia major omni laude
>   nec laudare sufficis.

The delightful English example : Ichot a burde in boure bryht (Wright's *Specimens*, No. XVI), is famous for its refrain :

Blow, northerne wynd,
Send þou me my suetyng
Blow, northerne wynd,
Blou, blou, blou.

The variety of the experimentation, practised during this period, is well exemplified in such MSS. as the Vernon and the Harleian. Northern France had produced stanzas of some complexity, particularly its *rondets*, *ballettes*, and *virelis*. In England, the appearance of two fixed forms has already been noted, the Octovian and the tail-rhymed stanza, the latter varying in the number of its lines from six to twelve, or from eight to sixteen, with some variety in the length of the lines themselves. Examples of various types of tail-rhymed stanza may be found in the Thornton romances. Ballad-stanza (abcb) had been anticipated as far back as Orm, and simple four-lined cross-rhyme in the *Bestiary*. A more complicated type is provided by *Sir Tristrem*, in which eight three-beat lines cross-rhymed are succeeded by a *bob* and an unrhymed *wheel* of two lines. *Sir Tristrem* dates from the end of the thirteenth century, and so provides a partial anticipation of the scheme of *Sir Gawayne and the Grene Knight*. The intense little satire, *Against the pride of ladies*, has a two-lined rhyming wheel preceded by a *bob*, and the *Song on the execution of Sir Simon Fraser* (1306) a three-lined wheel (aab), of which the last line echoes the *bob*. The *Hours of the Cross* (Vernon MS. No. 19) consists of a mono-rhymed stanza of four lines, followed by a three-lined wheel: in this case, the first line echoes the *bob*, the remainder constituting a couplet. The mono-rhymed section is an interesting continuation of Latin and French tradition: we come upon it again in Wright's *Specimens* Nos. 16, 25, 31 and 32, and in the *Song against the king of Almaigne*, where it is associated with a permanent refrain. In France, Colin Muset had already shown himself a prac-titioner in this type, and there was the tremendous example of the *Dies Irac* to serve as a permanent model:

Tuba mirum spargens sonum
per sepulchra regionum
coget omnes ante thronum.

Besides all this, novelties like the combined octaves and quatrains of the *Song of the Husbandmen*, the alliterative rhyming lines of the *Song against retinues*, the irregular stanzas (11 or 13 lines) of poems like *Middelerd for mon wes mad*, and so on, serve to prove the metrical ingenuity of the period.

A pendant to the vigorous denunciation of the political poems is supplied by the comic satire of the *Land of Cockaygne*, where geese fly in ready roasted and monks imbibe from rivers of wine. The contrasted picture of Paradise,

þer nis mete bote frute ;
þer nis halle, bure, no benche,
Bot watir, manis þurst to quenche.
Beþ þer no man but two,—
Hely and Enok also :
Elinglich may hi go
Whar þer woniþ men no mo,

serves as an introduction to the Rabelaisian delights of Cockaygne. A note of perennial interest recurs in the Middle English " Ubi sunt " poems, responsible for some charming things. Anticipations had appeared in the lyric passage of the pre-Conquest *Wanderer* :

Hwǣr cwōm mearg, hwǣr cwōm mago ? hwǣr cwōm maþ-þumgyfa ?
hwǣr cwōm symbla gesetu ? hwǣr sindon seledrēamas ?,

and in the famous lines of the 10th metre of *Boethius*. There were also Latin models like the

Dic ubi Salamon, olim tam nobilis ?

of Walter Map. In Middle English, versions occur in the *Sayings of St. Bernard*, in *Death*, and elsewhere, the outstanding example being the *Luue Ron* of Thomas of Hales :

>Hwer is Paris and Heleyne
>þat weren so bryht and feyre on bleo ?

But it is in the love poems that the finest examples of Middle English lyric are to be found,—in *Sumer is icumen in, Alison, Lenten ys come wiþ love to toune,* etc.,—and in the carols, anticipatory of the great fifteenth-century outburst. Here was material enough to prepare for Chaucer and, his work accomplished, for the great sixteenth-century lyrical revival.

XVI. THE METRICAL ROMANCES.

The popularity of the metrical romances during the Middle English period is attested by the *Cursor Mundi* (*c.* 1300) and Chaucer's *Sir Thopas.* The former attempts a kind of classification, beginning with the three famous " matters " of antiquity, of France, and of Britain : then follow, in a group, *Yonec, Isumbras, Amadas and Ydoine,* the list concluding with :

>Storis als o sere kin thinges
>O princes, prelates, and o kynges,
>Sanges sere of selcuth rime,
>Inglis, Frankys, and Latine.

It is noteworthy that no English version of *Yonec* exists, and that the extant *Sir Isumbras* and *Sir Amadace* belong to the latter part of the fourteenth century. It is, therefore, probable that the references are to French, rather than native, versions.

The predominance of France in the department of romance has already been illustrated. There are, however, indications that the English had advanced some distance in the art of story-telling before they came into intimate contact with the Normans. The Old English *Apollonius of Tyre* was a definite experiment in prose fiction, whatever its ultimate origin. More important still, there is reason to believe that the nucleuses of *Horn* and *Havelok* date back to the period of the Danish invasions. Other romances, like *Hereward* and *Waldef*, carry us back to the latter part of the eleventh century, and, no doubt, existed in English forms before they were translated into Norman-French.

Havelok and *Horn* are essentially viking romances, celebrating hard fighting, and lacking the sentimentalities of certain schools of romance. The hero of the former is a Danish king's son, of the latter the son of a king of Suddene or South Denmark. Both undergo treacherous treatment, Havelok being kept out of his own by the evil-disposed Godard, though he is saved by the fisherman Grim, eventually marries an English princess, and comes, at the same time, to his own in Denmark. Horn's enemy is his quondam friend, Fikenhild. While his native land is overrun by "Saracens," Horn is set in a boat and drifts to Ireland, where he first beholds Rymenhild. Fikenhild betrays Horn to the Irish king, and, for seven years, he suffers banishment, to return, in the end, to Ireland and to Rymenhild. Both romances abound in folk-lore and semi-historic material. In *Havelok*, we have the typical folk-story of the adventures of a king's son in the capacity of a kitchen-boy, until his noble birth is revealed by a magic sign : in *Horn*, recognition by means of a talisman. The historic basis of *Havelok* has been traced to the tenth century, to the adventures of Anláf Cuaran, driven from his heritage by his uncle, Æthelstan, and to the disinheriting of Ælfwynn (Goldeboru) by her uncle, Edward the Elder. In Gaimar's version, Anláf Cuaran has stepped into the place of his uncle, Reginwald (who aided Ælfwynn), and Æthelstan (or Edelsi) into that of his father, Edward the Elder. The Celtic names, Argentille and Orwain (Goldeboru and her mother), have displaced Ælfwynn and Æthelflæd. As for Horn, he may be identical with the viking Horm, who, in the ninth century, visited Cearbhall of Ireland to secure his assistance against the Lochlanns or Norwegians.

These verse-romances constitute part of a well-defined group dealing with native legend, a group further strengthened by the addition of *Beues of Hamtoun, Guy of Warwick, Athelston, Richard Cœur de Lion* and *Gamelyn.* The characteristic features throughout are vigorous action, unconventionality combined with a good deal of crudity of manners, and a complete absence of sentimentalism. Combats with "Saracens," giants, boars and dragons abound. The hero has his lady,—Rimenhild, Josian, Felice, or Goldborough,—but the dalliance of love fails to hold him. The extant text of *Horn* contains, indeed, two heroines of different types, Reynild and Rymenhild, but it is probable that the latter owes her origin to the ingenuity of some later and more sentimental writer. The mixture of old and new naturally varies with the dates of the poems. *Horn* is, generally, very primitive and contains a curious animistic element, illustrated in the following lines :

> Schup, bi the se flode,
> Daies haue thu gode :
> Bi the se brinke
> No water the nadrinke :
> ȝef thu cume to Suddene
> Gret thu wel al myne kenne.

But *Athelston* blunders over the account of the ordeal by fire and exhibits a confused history and geography. *Beues of Hamtoun,* though full of primitive vigour, is overlaid with adventure in the far East, while *Guy of Warwick* has supplemented its historical material, arising out of the struggle with the Danes in the tenth century, by a spiritless record of pilgrimage. Into *Richard Cœur de Lion* a large element of romance has intruded : but the grim humour and brutality of manners, characteristic of the older poems, is well illustrated in the incident of the Saracen's head. Of the romances comprising this group, *Waldef* and *Hereward* are extant only in French and Latin versions : while *Horn, Havelok, Guy,* and *Beues* exist in both English and French.

Oriental romance is exemplified by *Floris and Blanche-flur,* one of the earliest experiments of its kind in English. The numerous versions, French, Italian, Spanish, German, and Scandinavian, attest the vogue of the story in the West. A prose version, much altered and expanded, though scarcely to the benefit of the original, appeared in the fourteenth century in Boccaccio's *Filocolo.* In France, both an aristocratic and a popular rendering existed, to the former of which the English bears a close relationship. *Floris and Blancheflur* is a charming story of devoted love. From the outset, where Floris asks weeping,

> " Ne shal not Blancheflour lerne with me ?
> Ne can I noght to scole goon
> Without Blancheflour," he saide than,
> " Ne can I in no scole sing ne rede
> Without Blancheflour," he seide,

to the closing scene, in which their mutual tenderness overcomes the sultan, we feel the author's complete sympathy with the children's fate.

> For Floris was so fair yongling
> And Blancheflour so swete thing.

The triumph of love is charmingly exemplified in the *naïveté* of this old-world story.

The *motif* of a reunion of kindred associates in a single group a number of romances of various dates, *Isumbras, Eglamour, Torrent of Portugal, Octovian,* and *Triamour.* The first is, more particularly, a variant of the Eustace legend and a study of knightly patience. As a punishment for pride, Isumbras was separated from his wife and children, and subjected to severe penance, from which he emerged happily only after many years. This trial

E.L.C.   I

of patience by an accumulation of suffering imparts a curiously mediæval tone to the romance. *Eglamour*, while differing from *Isumbras* in many particulars, contains the separation and reunion motives. At the outset, Eglamour performs three mighty feats by slaying, in succession, a giant, a boar and a dragon. His lady, Cristabelle, had meantime been committed to the waves, in much the same way as Constance in the *Man of Lawe's Tale*. Later, Cristabelle married Degrabel, without recognising him as her son. The conflict between father and son, at the close, is a familiar incident in epic and romance. *Torrent of Portugal* is closely related to *Eglamour* and, possibly, a direct working-over of this latter. It has little merit, and is typical of the kind of thing that provoked Chaucer's smile in *Sir Thopas*. The number of identical rhymes suggests that the text has come down in a corrupt condition. The allusion to Wayland is interesting, if only by reason of its rarity. *Octovian* exists in two versions, a Northern and a Southern, of which the latter displays a distinctly *bourgeois* tone, the "humours" of Clement constituting the main attraction of this piece. The metre of the Southern version contrasts with that of the remaining pieces in this section, which are all in twelve-line tail-rhymed stanza. The so-called Octovian stanza, as found in this version, is illustrated in this following passage, in which Clement encourages his foster-child :

> He cryde : " Boy, ley on, with yre
> Strokes as ys woned thy syre !
> He ne fond neuer boon ne lyre
>   Hys ax with-stent,
> That he ne smot thorgh ech a swyre
>   Ryght at oo dent."

In *Triamour*, the adventures of the slandered queen, Margaret, in company with the old knight Roger and the faithful hound, are well told. After seven years by Roger's grave, the hound returned to court and killed the steward,

who had defamed his mistress. As the author naïvely
remarks, " Grete kyndenes ys in howndys ! " Later on,
Triamour, Margaret's son, overturned his father in a
joust and married the fair Helen.

Other romances, dealing with various aspects of the
knightly character, are less easy to classify. *Degrevant*,
in sixteen-line tail-rhymed stanzas, is an ingeniously
contrived love-story. The hero challenges the earl, who
raided his lands during his absence in the Holy Land.
He gets a glimpse of the earl's daughter on the castle-wall,
and falls in love. He pays many secret visits to the castle,
defends himself vigorously when discovered, and, finally,
wins Melydore's hand. Though not of outstanding poetic
merit, the romance abounds in interesting material, of
which much might have been made by a more skilful
writer. Degrevant's fight against odds is thus described :

> Whan thei syre Degrivaunt mett,
> Seven sperus one hym y-sett
> Evene in hys bassonett
>   Brasten a-two.
> Some baren hym thorw the gowne,
> Some brast one hys haberjowne ;
> Hys sqwyere was borne downe,
>   Hys swerd cast hym fro !
> Then syre Degrivaunt lygth,
> And rescowede hys knygth,
> And cryed to hym an hygth,
>   " Why wolt thou lyen so ? "
> The beste stedes that thei hade
> By the scholders he them scharde,
> He was never so hard y-stade
>   Ffor wele ne for wo !

Generydes exists in two versions, in couplets and rhyme-
royal. It is a late romance, betraying Chaucerian
influence. The adventures take place at the court of
Persia and elsewhere in the East. Generydes saves
his face with the Sultan by defeating his enemy, King
Bellyns. Clarionas, the Sultan's daughter, who has been

carried away to Egypt, is ultimately rescued by Generydes, disguised as a leper. In the end, Generydes
marries Clarionas and succeeds the Sultan on his death.
Parthenope, again in two versions, is a story of relationships between a mortal and a fairy lover. The French
original is extant. The fairy, Melior, has accepted
Parthenope, on condition that she shall remain invisible
for two and a half years. Though Parthenope fails to
keep the compact, he is aided by the lady's sister and
ultimately restored to favour. The influence of the
Cupid and Psyche story is possible. In the following
lines, the first appearance of the lady is described :

> And as he was in thys affraye,
> And hys herte fulle nere quappynge,
> In the flore he herde comynge
> A thynge fulle softely what euer hyt were,
> Whereoff fully he gan to fere.
> Meruayle he had what hyt myght be.
> " Allas the tyme," then sayde he,
> " That euer I was of woman bore,
> For welle I wotte I am butte lore."
> Under the clothys he can hym hyde,
> And drow hym to the beddys syde,
> Wenyng hyt had ben sum euylle thynge
> That he herde in the flore comynge.

Ipomydon is a noteworthy rendering of an Anglo-
French romance, composed in the twelfth century by
Hue de Rotelande. The material is composite, and
includes several motives familiar to romance. The
account of the three-days' tournament, for example,
reappears in *Lancelot*, and there are parallels for the
story of the Fair Unknown. The couplet version, printed
by Weber, is more condensed, but inferior. Lastly, the
Squire of Low Degree, told with much delicacy, despite its
imitative quality, contains many interesting technical
passages, and, at least, two unforgettable lines :

> It was a squyer of lowe degre
> That loved the kings doughter of Hungre.

Amis and Amiloun and *Sir Amadace* have been appropriately named romances of friendship. In the former, the tie of sworn brotherhood is strong enough to induce Amiloun to become a leper rather than fail his friend. In his turn, Amis sacrifices his children to save Amiloun. The knightly oath is made absolutely binding. Nor may the knight soil his honour : otherwise, Amis might have been expected to fight out his own quarrel with the treacherous steward. The workmanship of the poem is not first-rate, though the material is excellent. The character of Belisaunt does not appeal at the outset, but she displays heroic quality in the supreme test of the sacrifice of her children. Amiraunt, the devoted companion of Amiloun's exile, is sympathetically drawn. The story was highly popular in the Middle Ages, and reached England, probably, through an Anglo-Norman medium. In *Sir Amadace* the grateful dead *motif* appears. In return for his kindness to a widow, Amadace is relieved, in his own distress, by a White Knight, who stipulates for half of whatever he shall afterwards win. After Amadace's marriage, the White Knight appears and claims his share of wife and child. The hand of the slayer is arrested at the crucial moment, the White Knight revealing himself as the spirit of the grateful dead. As in the preceding romance, great emphasis is laid upon the sanctity of the oath. *Amadas and Ydoine* has sometimes been regarded as the source of the English romance, but love appears to have been the prominent element in this French version. The didactic note, characteristic of these latter romances, is prominent once more in *Roberd of Cisyle*, a product of the late fourteenth century. Pride brings about Robert's downfall : he degenerates into a court-fool, and is restored only after full confession of sin.

There remain to be mentioned the so-called Breton romances, the most attractive of all the groups in this section. Their ultimate origin has been sought in the Breton *lai*, a somewhat intangible thing, best represented by the work of Marie de France. The romances themselves make frequent reference to these *lais*, and, in the prologues to *Sir Orfeo* and *Lai le Freine*, there is a definite attempt to characterise them :

> We redeth oft, and findeth ywrite,
> And this clerkes wele it wite,
> Layes that ben in harping
> Ben yfounde of ferli thing :
> Sum bethe of wer, and sum of wo,
> Sum of joie and mirthe also,
> And sum of trecherie and of gile,
> Of old aventours that fel while ;
> And sum of bourdes and ribaudy,
> And many ther beth of fairy ;
> Of al thinges that men seth,
> Maist o loue forsothe thai beth.

In their final forms, the English romances appear to fall within the fourteenth century. In more than half the instances, the original couplet is preserved, while the remainder employ the tail-rhymed stanza. The themes are various and frequently paralleled elsewhere. *Lai le Freine* is an early version of the Griselda-story, and contains some excellent descriptive matter, such as the account of the moonlight walk to the convent. *Emare* is a variant of the Constance-saga, of which Chaucer made use in the *Man of Lawe's Tale* : the Mercian Offa-saga represents a pre-conquest version. *Sir Degare* is a combination of many *motifs*, the *lai* element being most clearly evident in the castle-episode. A strange amalgam of history, folk-lore, and legend constitutes the matter of the *Earl of Toulouse*, while the familiar ecclesiastical story of Robert the Devil is re-told in *Sir Gowther*. The most attractive members of this group, *Sir Launfal* and *Sir Orfeo*, deal with the supernatural. The old-world story of Orpheus and Eurydice becomes a thing of rare charm in its new setting. The lady, Heurodis, spirited away by the king of faery, is ultimately won back by her husband's minstrelsy :

Allas ! to long last mi liif,
When Y no dar nought with mi wiif,
No hye to me o word speke,
Allas ! whi nil min hert breke !
Parfay, quath he, tide what bitide,
Whider so this leuedi ride,
The selue way I chil streche,
Of liif ne deth me no reche.

Sir Launfal has won the love of the faery-queen, Triamour, but is on the point of losing her forever, in consequence of his broken pledge, when she appears to justify him :

Thus Launfal, wythouten fable,
That noble knyght of the rounde table,
Was take yn to fayrye ;
Seththe saw hym yn thys lond no man,
Ne no more of hym telle I ne can,
For sothe, wythout lye.

XVII. ROBERT OF GLOUCESTER TO BARBOUR

The fourteenth century has been styled the age of nationalism in contrast with its predecessor, the age of scholasticism. During this period, the struggle between native English and alien French gradually came to an end, and resulted, after 1350, in the ousting of French from the schools. The period is distinguished by the revival of the old alliterative line and by the recognition of independent authorship, though there are a number of unnamed writers, in particular the *Pearl*-poet, the compiler of the *Robin Hood* cycle, and the comic author of the Towneley *Shepherds' play*, who rank among the greatest. In this section, we are concerned with those named authors of the century, who fall within the period

1300 to 1375, and, thus, take rank among the predecessors, or early contemporaries, of Chaucer.

Robert of Gloucester was an important practitioner in that type of rhymed chronicle, which became familiar after the disappearance of the Anglo-Saxon prose variety. The first to attempt the new style was Layamon, whose *Brut,* dated *c.* 1205, is a record of events from the days of Troy to the death of Caedwalla, in 689. A third of the space is devoted to Arthur, whose exploits are handled with the dignity of the epic writer. Layamon is interested less in " romancing " than in records of conquest. He is, by turns, dramatic, vigorous and realistic. But there are elements of mystery, for which he was, perhaps, indebted to a text of Wace, into which Breton material had been incorporated. In the wake of Layamon followed Robert of Gloucester, whose *Chronicle* is extant in two texts. Except for occasional interpolations, these agree down to the death of Henry I (1135), when they begin to diverge. The first recension, which is four times as lengthy as its successor, recounts the events of 1216–1272 with much detail. It has been conjectured that these recensions were of separate authorship, and that the nucleus, down to 1135, represents an independent poem. The name " Robert " is introduced, however, into the longer recension in connection with the Battle of Evesham (1265) ; there is also a reference to the canonisation of St. Lewis in 1297, and local data connected with Gloucestershire. The traditional association of the author with Gloucester is, thus, upheld. But the reference to Henry I, in the earlier section, as " ure King that we abbeth nou," rules out Robert, though he may, possibly, have revised this older material. The shorter recension, again, points to Gloucester as its place of origin. The authorities employed in the first part of the poem were Geoffrey of Monmouth, Henry of Huntingdon, and the *Life of St. Kenelm.* The genealogy of Brutus appears to have been drawn from Geoffrey, the account of the foundation of Glastonbury from William of Malmesbury, and that of the reign of Edward the Confessor from Ailred of Rievaux. Later on, material was derived from the Winchester and the Waverley *Annals*, the metrical *Lives of the Saints*, and elsewhere. Robert of Gloucester was an undistinguished, though patriotic, poet. He handled his rhymed septenars with facility, and proved the capabilities of the metre for narrative purposes. He deserves the title of chronicler, if only for his impartiality and enthusiasm for the truth ; his scepticism in Arthurian matters contrasts strangely with the credulity of the romancers, reminding us of Caxton's hesitation in view of assertions that at Dover " ye may see Gawaine's skull." Robert's influence has been detected in the Royal MS. of the *Short Metrical Chronicle* (South-West Midland), but the unprinted *Chronicle* of Thomas Bek relies upon Geoffrey of Monmouth throughout, at least, the whole of its opening section.

A sub-division of the political literature of the period consists of prophetic writings, anticipations of which had appeared in Geoffrey of Monmouth's *Merlin*. The somewhat shadowy personality of Thomas of Erceldoun, who died before the end of the thirteenth century, is associated with various mysterious utterances, among which was an apparent forecast of the death of Alexander III, in 1285. In the fourteenth century Adam Davy, marshal of Stratford-atte-Bowe, composed five visions concerning Edward II, which are assigned to the king's reign (1307–1327). Adam Davy has no claim to distinction, though his lines run fairly smoothly. His visions have linguistic interest, however, as early specimens of the London dialect.

With Robert Mannyng of Brunne we revert to the chronicle, extending, in this case, from Noah to Edward I, the first part in short couplets, the second in rhymed alexandrines. Wace, Pierre de Langtoft, and Bede were the chief authorities drawn upon. The *Chronicle* was finished in 1338, thirty-five years after the *Handlyng Synne*, but the earlier work, as it happens, possesses the

greater interest. It is addressed to the Gilbertine community at Sempringham :

> Dan Philipp was mayster þat tyme
> þat I began þis ynglysche ryme
> þe yeer of grace fil þan to be
> A/mccc and þre.

The framework consists of a series of discourses upon
the Ten Commandments, the Seven Deadly Sins, the
Seven Sacraments, the twelve requisites and graces of
confession, each point being illustrated by an accompanying *exemplum* or story. The book is, accordingly, a
collection of tales, all the more valuable in that they
illustrate the social life of the period in every grade.
Thus, the sin of sloth is exemplified by the rich man,
ill-disposed to rise for church on Sunday mornings, the
sin of pride by certain young bucks, a prey to every new
fashion. Among the stories, those of the Cambridge
miser, who died in the attempt to swallow his silver, of
Piers the usurer and his redemption, of the bear that
guarded St. Florens' sheep and was slain by the envious
monks, of the mother who cursed her child,—these will
serve to illustrate the variety of Robert's style. Everywhere there are allusions to the occupations and amuse-
ments of the people,—their fairs, miracle-plays, dances,
carols, etc.,—with abundant warnings as to the risks
incurred. Robert's interest in the common folk constitutes his great claim on our gratitude :

> For lewde men I undyr-toke
> On englyssh tunge to make þys boke.

Handlyng Synne is far from being a mere translation,
since, in dealing with Waddington's text, Robert everywhere permitted himself freedom. His original stories,
of which there are quite a dozen, were selected with
special reference to general edification. Robert was
interested in popular songs and romances and, in his
Chronicle, supplied an original contribution to the *Havelok*
legend :

Men sais in Lyncoln castelle ligges ʒit a stone,
That Havelok kast wele forbi euer ilkone,
And ʒit the chapelle standes ther he weddid his wife,
Goldeburgh, the Kynges douhter, that saw is ʒit rife.
And of Gryme a fisshere, men redes ʒit in ryme,
That he bigged Grymesby Gryme that ilk tyme.

The religious poet, William of Shoreham, shares material
in common with Robert Mannyng, three of his poems
being devoted to the Seven Sacraments, the Ten Commandments, and the Seven Deadly Sins. He also wrote
two Virgin poems, the *Joys of the Virgin*, and a *Hymn
to Mary*, the latter translated, according to the colophon,
from Grosseteste. William differed, however, from Mannyng in making his appeal to a more cultured audience ;
he was less concerned with the elements of faith than
with such abstruse points of doctrine, as he interprets
in his poem on the Trinity, the Creation, and the Temptation. William of Shoreham is interesting by reason of
his varied metres. He wrote in the short stanza, abab, in
rime couée, and in a six-lined stanza of the form, aabccb.
A favourite metre was his seven-lined stanza, abcbded,
and he experimented, further, in the form abcbdbeb.

The great fourteenth-century mystic, Richard Rolle,
ranks among the outstanding figures of the period.
After a brief sojourn at Oxford, he began his romantic
career by suddenly assuming hermit's attire and settling
on the estate of Sir John Dalton in the Yorkshire North
Riding. His residence there was not permanent, and,
after some four years of contemplative existence, he
began his wanderings from place to place, taking a share
in the religious controversies of the day. He then
settled in the neighbourhood of Anderby, in close proximity to another recluse, Margaret Kirby, and continued
his controversial writings. In his last period, we find
him at Hampole in South Yorkshire, associated, till his
death, with a Cistercian nunnery, apparently in the
capacity of spiritual adviser.

Rolle's appearance at Oxford coincided with the last

phase of the scholastic triumph : his own method, henceforth, was the very antithesis of Scotism. In the *Incendium Amoris,* he describes the last phases of his spiritual development as *calor, canor, dulcor.* The *canor,* otherwise defined as *musica spiritualis, invisibilis melodia, sonus cœlestis, iubilatio,* is a state of rapture, in which the dominant element is love-melody. In several respects, Rolle was opposed to the monastic systems of his day ; he recognized no authority beyond that of contemplative love, actuated by will :

Caritas nunquam est nisi in bona voluntate, nec bona voluntas nisi in caritate.

Consequently, he came into violent opposition with the established orders, and failed, at the same time, to win acceptance for his asceticism among the commonalty. Though the canon of his writings is unsettled, it is clear that, in his prose, he carried on the ornate tradition of Old English, with its impassioned, rhythmical melody :

þou þat lyste lufe, herken and here of luf. In þe sang of luf it es writen : " I slepe and my hert wakes." Mykel lufe he schewes þat never is irk to lufe, bot ay, standand, sittand, gangand or wirkand, es ay his lufe thynkand, and oft-syth þarof dremande. Forþi þat I lufe, I wow þe, þat I myght have þe als I walde, noght to me bot to my lorde. (Horstmann, I, 50.)

The *Pricke of Conscience,* a monitory poem dealing in an abstract way with the wretchedness of man upon earth and with future punishments and rewards, has long been associated with Rolle, on the authority of Lydgate, but is now considered doubtfully his. Rolle has to his credit, however, several poems which entitle him to a pioneer position among English hymn-writers :

Unkynde man, gif kepe til me
and loke what payne I suffer for þe.
Synful man, on þe I cry,
alanly for þi lufe I dy.

Rolle is to be judged as a mystic rather than as a philosopher. He left to his successor, Walter Hilton, the logical ordering of his doctrine, and to the leaders of the Reformation the enforcing of those rights of individual conscience, for which he himself had stood.

Not much can be said in praise of the *Ayenbite of Inwyt*, translated, in 1340, by Dan Michel of Northgate from Friar Lorens' *Le somme des vices et des vertues*. Its general scheme relates it to the *Handlyng Synne* and the *Pricke of Conscience*, but the obscurity of its style and its inept workmanship set it in a class below these. Its value is almost exclusively linguistic, as a specimen of the Middle Kentish dialect.

The poems of Lawrence Minot bring us, in their revised form, to the middle of the century. Minot lived on the borderland between the Northern and Midland areas, and, in his rhymes, employed varying dialectal forms. Nothing is known of him beyond his name, which he introduces twice into his poems. His subjects are the battle of Halidon Hill (1333), Edward III's invasion of France and entry into Brabant (1338–1339), the naval battle of Sluys (1340), the sieges of Tournay (1340) and of Calais (1346), the battle of Crécy (1346), Neville's Cross (1346), the naval battle with the Spaniards (1350), and the capture of Guisnes (1352). These events are described with spirit and vigour, but without literary distinction. Minot was a whole-hearted supporter of Edward III, his poetical creed being distinguished chiefly by animosity against the foreigner. He had, at all events, the salt of patriotism in his veins. Minot's stanzas are varied, and interesting as experiments. He tried *rime couée* (4), six-lined alliterative stanzas aaaabb (2, 5, 9, 10, 11), four-beat couplets (3, 7), the form abcbabab, with either three or four beats (1, 6), and finally ababbcbc (7, 8). In several poems, the stanzas are linked as in the *Pearl* and, similarly, individual lines, in 2 and 5 :

Whare er ȝe, Skottes of Saint Johnes towne ?
þe boste of ȝowre baner es betin all doune ;
When ȝe bosting will bede Sir Edward es boune
For to kindel ȝow care and crak ȝowre crowne :
  He has crakked ȝowre croune, wele worth þe while,
  Schame bityde þe Skottes for þai er full of gile.

The poems of John Barbour were composed in a still
more Northerly dialect, the Scots of Aberdeen. As in
the case of Chaucer, Barbour's life has been reconstructed
out of official records. In 1357, he set out for Oxford
under a royal safe-conduct, in which he is referred to as
Archdeacon of Aberdeen. In the same year, he figured
as one of three procurators appointed to determine the
ransom of David II. He was in England again in 1364–1365,
and abroad in France in 1368. Entries in the exchequer
rolls, extending from 1373–1384, make it clear that he
acted, during this period, as auditor of the Exchequer
(compotorum auditor). He received a grant of £10 in
March 1377, a pension of 20 shillings in August 1378,
and, in 1388, a further pension of £10. He appears to
have died in 1395, five years before Chaucer.

Wyntoun is the authority for Barbour's authorship of
the *Bruce*, but there is no evidence that he meant to
associate him with a *Brut*, also. The *Stewartis original*,
to which Wyntoun refers, is now lost. It appears to
have been an attempt to trace the genealogy of the
Stewarts to Banquo, and, ultimately, to Ninus. The
scribal insertion in the Camb. MS. of Lydgate's *Siege of
Troy*,

  Here endis Barbour and begynnis þe monk,

is of doubtful authenticity, though the Scottish *Lives
of the Saints* in the same MS. may, possibly, be connected
with Barbour. They are composed in his metre and
dialect, and include accounts of two saints, associated
with Aberdeen.

Barbour's aim, in the *Bruce*, was to combine profit
with pleasure :

Storys to rede ar delitabill,
Suppos that thai be nocht bot fabill :
Than suld storys that suthfest wer,
And thai war said on gud maner,
Have doubill plesance in heryng.

The poem is, accordingly, of considerable historical value, despite its atmosphere of romance. Barbour's literary instincts are attested by his references, sometimes lengthy, to Guido, the Machabees, Alexander, Julius Cæsar, Arthur, Fingal, Hannibal, etc. He, also, recounts how Robert Bruce beguiled the time on the shores of Loch Lomond by reading *Ferumbras* aloud to his men. Barbour's hero-worship accounts for the epic strain in his poem ; his humour, where it breaks forth, is also of this type :

He maid thame na gud fest, perfay,
And nocht-for-thi yneuch had thai.
For thouch thame failit of the met,
I warne yhow weill thai war weil! wet.

The narrative is well sustained throughout, with an occasional striking passage, such as the accounts of the fire at Kildrummy, of the shining hosts of Sir Aymer, and of the approach of spring in Book V :

This wes in vere, quhen wyntir tyde,
With his blastis hydwis to byde,
Wes ouerdriffin : and byrdis smale,
As thristill and the nychtingale,
Begouth rycht meraly to syng,
And for to mak in thair synging
Syndry notis, and soundis sere,
And melody plesande to here.
And the treis begouth to ma
Burgeonys, and brycht blumys alsua,
To wyn the heling of thair hevede
That wikkit wyntir had thame revede.

XVIII. THE ALLITERATIVE ROMANCES

The alliterative romances constitute one of the most attractive products of the Middle English period. As a literary phenomenon, they represent a highly curious reversion to pre-Conquest methods, with certain modifications consequent upon their date of composition. The old alliterative line, remodelled and less restricted, makes a reappearance, together with much of the old epic phraseology and the old epic humour. The enthusiasm, with which battle and sea-passages are handled, links these poems of the Middle English period with their Anglian predecessors, but the culture represented is a product of the new period, a period of amalgamation between Englishman and Norseman and Frenchman. Together with the old enthusiasm for nature in her wilder aspects, a delight in hunting and architecture, in decorative material and precious stones, makes itself felt. The effects of the Early Renaissance are apparent in the choice of subjects, while the vocabulary displays a large French element, side by side with the native English and Norse. Of the authorship of these poems practically nothing is known : they belong, without exception, to the North West Midland, or to the Northern area ; in other words, to the Celtic borderland. It has been conjectured that the old alliterative line had lived on in popular speech throughout the period of French domination, but the problem as to how the old epic manner came to be revived in this particular area during the second half of the fourteenth century is less easy of solution.

The earliest products of the school, *William of Palerne* and *Joseph of Arimathie*, belong apparently to c. 1350. It is known that the former was translated from the French, at the command of Sir Humphrey de Bohun, who died in 1361. The legend of the werwolf is widely distributed. William, a son of the king of Apulia, was saved from a treacherous uncle by a werwolf, who turned out to be a transformed prince of Spain. The boy became page to the Emperor of Rome's daughter, with whom he afterwards took to flight. The adventures in the forest form the most attractive side of the book. The matter is largely that of the love romance and strangely different from that of most other poems of this school. The extant *Guillaume de Palerne*, a sophisticated poem in couplets, presents the nearest parallel. The passage, in which the child, summoned to court, sends a parting message to his forest friends, will serve to illustrate the style of the English version :

And gode sire for Godes love　　　also greteth wel oft
Alle my freyliche felawes　　　　that to this forest longes :
Han pertilyche in many places　　pleide with ofte
Hugonet and Huet　　　　　　that hende litel dwerg
And Abelot and Martynet　　　　Hugones gaie sons
And the cristen Akarin　　　　　that was mi kyn fere
And the trewe kinnesman　　　　the payenes sone
And alle other frely felawes　　　that thou faire knawes
That God mak hem gode men　　for his mochel grace.

In *Joseph of Arimathie* the ecclesiastical origin and wonder-working properties of the Grail are set forth. It miraculously sustained Joseph during his forty years' imprisonment, and enabled him afterwards to convert Vespasian and the King of Sarras. Further, the king was saved from his enemy, Tholomer of Babylon, by the shield which Joseph presented to him. Joseph's career ultimately ended in Wales. The account of the battle with Tholomer is an example of the alliterative method, at its best.

The *Chevalere Assigne* belongs to the cycle of Godfrey of Bouillon, of which it is the sole representative in English before the fifteenth century. Exposed by the cruelty of the queen-mother, the seven children of king Oryens fell into the hands of a hermit. Round their necks they wore chains, which being severed, the children flew away in the form of swans. Helyas, having escaped transformation, returned to court and rescued his mother. The rest were ultimately restored by means of the chains, all save one. With this latter, Helyas sailed away, to be known, henceforth, as the Knight of the Swan. A fuller form of the story appeared in the sixteenth century, where we are informed of Godfrey of Bouillon's connection with this stock. A sober account of Godfrey's career was printed by Caxton in 1481. The penalty, exacted from Beatrice at the beginning of the Middle English version, is a folk-lore element, found again in *Lai le Freine*.

The *Gest Historiale of the Destruction of Troy*, the alliterative *Alexander* fragments, and *Titus and Vespasian* constitute a group of romances dealing with antiquity. Of these, the two former have already been referred to. The latter exists in an alliterative and a couplet version, both of which appear to be of French origin. Some dependence upon Josephus has been detected in the alliterative poem. To Titus and Vespasian fell the task of avenging the death of Christ, and the details of the siege of Jerusalem afforded ample scope for the poet's imagination. The legend of St. Veronica is introduced into the earlier part of the story.

The remaining representatives of alliterative romance,— the Thornton *Morte Arthure, Sir Gawayne and the Grene Knight*, the *Awntwyrs off Arthure at the Terne Wathelyne*, and *Golagros and Gawaine*,—constitute a highly important section of the Arthurian cycle. In the former, Gawain plays a prominent *rôle* : he is the central and dominating figure in the remainder. In fact, he was the only knight, associated with Arthur, round whom a separate cycle grew up in England.

The *Morte Arthure* belongs definitely to the lineage of Geoffrey. Some details appear to have been added from Layamon, or Wace, and there is more than one reference to a " cronycle " or " romance," as an authority. But the poem is distinguished by almost complete independence : to its predecessors it owes little beyond the general outline of Arthur's career. The *Morte Arthure* can scarcely be classed as a romance, in the sense that the term is employed of the Gawain poems. It is rather a serious chronicle, a record of dramatic situations and of deeds done, during that career of conquest that bore the king to Rome. The author has a lofty conception of his office, and maintains a strong didactic attitude. Mordred's treachery is foreshadowed in Arthur's dream, but the king is held responsible for his own misfortunes :

> Thow has schedde myche blode, and schalkes distroyede,
> Sakeles, in cirquytrie, in sere kynges landis ;
> Schryfe the of thy schame, and schape for thyne ende.

As for the more romantic elements of the Arthurian story,—the wizardry of Merlin, the mystic spell of the Grail, the loves of Lancelot and Guinevere,—these things are lacking. Nor is there any hint of mystery in connection with Arthur's death. The *Morte Arthure* is a strong composition, conceived in a spirit other than the romantic. The author has an eye for the detailed picturesque, an enthusiasm for heroic exploit, and a command of pathos well illustrated by the king's lament over the loss of Gawain :

> Than gliftis the gud kynge and glopyns in herte,
> Gronys full grisely with gretande teris ;
> Knelis down to the cors, and kaught it in armes,
> Kastys upe his umbrere, and kyssis hyme sone,
> Lokes one his eye-liddis, that lowkkide ware faire,
> His lippis like to the lede, and his lire falowede.
> Than the corownde kyng cryes fulle lowde :
> " Dere kosyne o kynde, in kare am I leuede !
> ffor nowe my wirchipe es wente, and my were endide.
> Here es the hope of my hele, my happynge of armes,
> My herte and my hardynes hale one hym lengede,
> My concell, my comforthe, that kepide myne herte.
> Of alle knyghtes the kynge that undir Criste lifede,
> Thou was worthy to be kynge, thofe I the corowne bare.
> My wele and my wirchipe of alle this werlde riche
> Was wonnene thowrghe sir Gawayne, and thourghe his witt
>   one.

The group of romances associated with Gawain are

peculiar in that they stand outside the direct line of Geoffrey of Monmouth. The *provenance* of these poems is somewhat obscure, though the ultimate starting-point lay, probably, in the distant Celtic background. In *Sir Gawayne and the Grene Knight* we have a combination of the beheading game with the chastity test. The former *motif* had found its earliest literary representation in the Old Irish tale of *Fled Bricrend* (assigned to the ninth century), and reappeared later, in the thirteenth century, in the continuation of the *Conte del Graal*, the *Perlesvaus*, *La mule sans frein*, *Humbaut*, and the German *Diu Krône*: the second appeared in the Old French *Ider*, certain Italian *canzoni* of the fourteenth century, and elsewhere. The original hero of the beheading game was the Irish prince, Cuchulainn, with whom Gawain shared several characteristics. In later versions, the beheading game was frequently combined with some kind of a test, as, indeed, is the case in *La mule sans frein* and the related *Diu Krône*. It is probable that the English poem followed the lines of some French romance, no longer extant.

Sir Gawayne and the Grene Knight has been claimed as the finest of the alliterative romances, a position mainly due to the skill with which the character of the central figure is portrayed. With Bedivere and Kay, Gawain belonged to the original nucleus of knights associated with Arthur : in origin, he was primarily Celtic. But, with the growth of the cycle, his *rôle* increased enormously. From an early period, he was closely associated with Guinevere, and the most generally respected of the Knights of the Table Round. Courtesy, prowess, sense of honour,—such were the qualities immediately associated with his name :

> Noble he was and curteis,
> Honour of him men rede and seis.

Unfortunately, a new view of Gawain's character was sanctioned by Malory in the *Morte D'Arthur*, whence the conception familiar from Tennyson's lines :

Light was Gawain in life, and light in death
Is Gawain, for the ghost is as the man.

In the fourteenth century, Gawain was still the knight
par excellence, the mirror of courtesy, and the soul of
honour. On the appearance of the Green Knight, he
eagerly accepted the challenge to cut off his head, and
when, to the general consternation, the knight recovered,
Gawain resolutely prepared to submit to a return blow
a year thence at the Green Chapel. The time passed
quickly, and the eve of his departure arrived. At this
point, an elaborate account of the arming of a mediæval
knight is introduced, the " pentangle " on Gawain's shield
being taken as symbolical of his particular virtues. The
journey to the Green Chapel led the knight by perilous
ways, from which he emerged on Christmas Eve at the
gate of the castle, the architecture of which is described
with an expert's enthusiasm. The jovial lord pressed
him to stay, and Gawain found himself lodged luxuriously.
His presence was regarded as an honour to the castle,
guest whispering to guest :

Now schal we semlych se sleʒteʒ of þewez,
And þe teccheles termes of talkyng noble,
Wich spede is in speche, unspurd may we lerne,
Syn we haf fonged þat fyne fader of nurture.

At the end of the Christmas festival, the lord returned
to the hunt, arranging with Gawain beforehand that the
latter should remain in his chamber, and that, at the
end of the day, each should exchange with the other the
products of his winning. Gawain, tempted by the
beautiful lady of the castle, was the recipient of several
kisses, which he religiously exchanged each night for the
products of the lord's chase. But he withheld a girdle,
which promised to keep him immune from danger. On
New Year's day, Gawain arrived at the Green Chapel,
and was struck by the wildness of the neighbourhood.
He flinched at the first blow, though but a feint, and was
reproached by the Green Knight. At the second feint,

he became angry and bade the knight "thrash on":

> Wy, þresch on, þou þro mon, þou þreteȝ to longe,
> I hope þat þi hert arȝe wyth þyn awen seluen.

The third time, he was slightly wounded in the neck. The Green Knight then explained that he was himself the lord of the castle, and that all that had happened had been in the nature of a test of Gawain's courage and chastity. He complimented him upon having emerged almost unscathed, but explained that the wound in the neck was the result of his error in concealing the girdle:

> Now know I wel þy cosses, and þy costes als,
> And þe wowyng of my wyf, I wroȝt hit myseluen;
> I sende hir to asay þe, and sothly me þynkkeȝ,
> On þe fautlest freke, þat ever on fote ȝede;
> As perle bi þe quite pese is of prys more,
> So is Gawayn, in god fayth, bi oþer gay knyȝteȝ.

Gawain retained the green girdle and, upon his return to court, this "band of blame" was adopted by the knights as the symbol of a new brotherhood.

It will be evident from the above *résumé* that *Sir Gawayne and the Grene Knight* is much more than a mere variant of the beheading story. The appointment at the Green Chapel is, indeed, kept constantly before the reader's mind, and the final scene constitutes a good climax: but the body of the poem is occupied with other matters, arising out of the combination of the two *motifs*. The scenes at Arthur's court after the departure of the Green Knight, Gawain's lonely journey through the realm of Logres and North Wales, his view of the castle from a distance, his reception by the lord, the stolen interviews with the lady on the following days, with the contrasting descriptions of the chase,—these things serve to bring out, not only the author's descriptive power and technical knowledge, but also his wonderful psychological insight. The emotional descriptions of wild nature would alone entitle him to a high position among mediæval poets, and he has, further, that detailed knowledge of dress and armour, of architecture and venery, characteristic of his school. Moreover, no poet of the period excelled him in knowledge of courtly diction and convention, and it would be difficult to find his peer in the handling of such delicate situations, as arose out of the stolen interviews at the castle :

"In goud faype," quod Gawayn, " God yow forȝelde,
Gret is þe gode gle, and gomen to me huge,
þat so worþy as ȝe wolde wynne hidere,
And pyne yow with so pouer a mon, as play wyth your knyȝt,
With any skynneȝ countenaunce, hit keuereȝ me ese ;
Bot to take þe toruayle to my-self, to trwluf expoun,
And towche þe temes of tyxt, and taleȝ of armeȝ,
To yow þat, I wot wel, weldeȝ more slyȝt
Of þat art, bi þe half, or a hundreth of seche
As I am, oþer euer schal, in erde þer I leue,
Hit were a fole fele-folde, my fre, by my trawþe.
I wolde yowre wylnyng worche at my myȝt,
As I am hyȝly bihalden, and ever-more wylle
Be seruaunt to your-seluen, so save me dryȝtyn ! "
þus hym frayned þat fre, and fondet hym ofte
Forto haf wonnen hym to woȝe, what-so scho poȝt elles,
Bot he defended hym so fayr, þat no faut semed,
Ne non euel on nawþer halue, nawþer þay wysten,
              bot blysse ;
       þay laȝed and layked longe,
       At þe last scho con hym kysse,
       Hire leu fayre con scho fonge,
       And went hir waye iwysse.

In the fifteenth century, there appeared, under the title of the *Grene Knight*, a *résumé* of our romance, in six-line tail-rhymed stanzas. This version dispenses with mystery, informing us, at the outset, that the Green Knight's name is Sir Bredbeddle, and afterwards identifying the castle as his. The author definitely associates the story with the foundation of the Order of the Bath. The *Turke and Gowin*, in the same metre, contains novel features,—Gawain sports with giants in an under-ground castle, and eventually disenchants the Turk by striking

off his head. In *Sir Gawene and the Carle of Carelyle*
(in twelve-line tail-rhymed stanzas) the carl puts Gawain's
obedience to the test, and, finding him reliable, repents
the number of victims he has slain and becomes a knight
of the Round Table.

Two alliterative romances remain to be characterised,
the *Awntyrs off Arthure at the Terne Wathelyne* and
Golagros and Gawain. The metre of these is identical,
and, curiously enough, both consist of two independent
parts. There are excellent combats ; in the one, between
Gawain and Galleroune, in the other, between Gawain
and Golagros. The first part of the *Awntyrs* is occupied
with a ghost which imparts moral counsel to Guinevere
at the Tarn Wadling. A source for this exists in the
Trental of St. Gregory. In *Golagros and Gawaine*, the
opening incident serves to contrast the courtesy of Gawain
with Kay's boorishness. The *Awntyrs* has been assigned
by some to the Scottish poet Huchoun, and *Golagros* to
the clerk of Tranent : but the geography of the former
points to Cumberland as its place of origin, and *Golagros*
may well have originated in the same district.

XIX. THE *PEARL*-POET AND HUCHOUN

No poet of the mediæval period has aroused more
enthusiasm among scholars during recent years than the
author of *Pearl.* His personality has been vigorously
debated, the canon of his works discussed, and, as in the
case of Cynewulf, hypothetical lives of the poet have
been written.

As far back as 1839, Sir Frederic Madden in his edition
of *Sir Gawayne* spoke with enthusiasm of the author's
gifts, and assigned to him not only the poem in question

but the three others in the MS. (Cotton Nero Ax + 4),— *Pearl, Patience,* and *Cleanness.* In his *Early English alliterative poems* (1864), Morris, while assuming common authorship, put forward the view that *Pearl* was an expression of the poet's " sorrow for the loss of his infant child, a girl of two years old." Ten Brink, in 1877, first attempted the hypothetical life, and, since that date, much has been written, particularly by Sir Israel Gollancz, who, entering into the spirit of the poems with fine insight and enthusiasm, has made this author peculiarly his own.

The alliterative poems in the Cotton Nero MS. occur in the order,—*Pearl, Cleanness, Patience,* and *Sir Gawayne,* and are accompanied by rough sketches, in which the author is depicted slumbering by a mound clad in a red gown with a blue hood, or standing by a stream with his hands raised to the opposite shore, or kneeling, while a lady extends her arm towards him from an embattled wall. Then follow sketches of Noah and his family, Daniel and Belshazzar, Jonah and the whale, and Jonah in Nineveh : lastly, scenes associated with the *Gawayne* romance. All this argues, if it does not prove, unity of authorship, and there is the further evidence of common vocabulary, style, and thought, e.g. *Pearl* 341–48 resembles *Patience* 5–8; *Cleanness* 523–27 presents a general likeness to *Gawayne* 500–30; while *Gawayne* 2364 reminds us of *Cleanness* 1068, 1157, and of the *Pearl,* in general. Attempts to determine the chronological order of the poems have varied slightly. Ten Brink placed *Sir Gawayne* first in order of time, and *Patience* last, but *Pearl,* with its highly elaborate metrical scheme, its abundant similes, and its general indebtedness to the allegorical school, may well have been the author's earliest effort. In the same way, Chaucer opened his career as an imitator of the French allegorists, before attaining to the independence of the *Canterbury Tales.*

The *Pearl* poet displays considerable reading and interest in curious lore. The *Vulgate* represents his main authority, but there is little to prove that he was

acquainted with patristic literature, as represented by the
De patientia, De Jona et Nineve, or the *De Sodoma* of
Tertullian. An interesting reference to " Clopyngel in
the compas of his clene rose " proves his acquaintance
with Jean de Meun, some of the details of the destruction
of Sodom derive probably from Mandeville, while a general
knowledge of French romance is attested by *Sir Gawayne.*
But it has scarcely been proved that he was acquainted
with Boccaccio, despite the resemblance between *Pearl* and
his Latin eclogue, *Olympia.* As regards native literature,
the symbolism in *Pearl* points clearly to the Virgin poetry
of the thirteenth and fourteenth centuries, though this
hardly justifies the conclusion that the poem, necessarily,
contains no autobiography. A highly interesting problem
concerns the author's theological position. It is probable
that the account of the state of the blessed, as described
in *Pearl*, derives from Bradwardine, and even marks an
advance upon his teaching : in the fourteenth century,
such doctrines, no doubt, savoured of heresy.

The metre of the poems merits particular attention ;
it represents, in general, a compromise between Old
English alliterative method and the principles of the
French school. *Pearl* is composed in twelve-lined stanzas
with a comparatively simple rhyme-scheme, ababababbcbc,
identical with that employed in many of the Vernon
poems. The stanza concludes with what is practically
a *refrain*, since the last line is echoed, in varying phrase,
throughout a whole section of, generally, five stanzas.
Further, the phrasing of the last line of each stanza is
caught up in the initial line of its successor, throughout
the whole poem. Thus, by means of alliteration, con-
catenation, and the device of the *refrain*, the poem is
welded, with marvellous ingenuity, into one artistic
and organic whole. As the poet progressed in strength,
he came to depend less upon adventitious aids. Assuming
Sir Gawayne to have been his next composition, he now
replaced the inter-laced stanza by the unrhymed *laisse*,
with concluding *bob* and *wheel*. In *Cleanness* and

Patience he dispensed entirely with rhyme, but employed the quatrain as the basis of his scheme.

The literary qualities of *Pearl* and its successors have attracted attention from the beginning. In the first place, a certain "high seriousness" is evinced in his choice of subject,—the chastity motive of *Sir Gawayne* with its stress upon honour, the commendation of innocence in *Pearl*, of purity and of resignation in its successors. This didactic intent serves to associate the poet with his Anglian predecessors, Cynewulf and the older epic writers, and is, by no means, the sole link, serving to prove organic connection between the Anglian and West Midland schools. The high imaginative qualities evinced in the nature-passages,—the winter-scene in *Sir Gawayne*, the storm in *Patience*, the war of the elements against the doomed cities in *Cleanness*,—are, indeed, additional proofs of this intimacy. Further, the poems are humanised by the sincerity of their passion : an intense emotion permeates *Pearl*, and, though the poet becomes gradually more objective, the personal note is still prominent in the prologues to the later poems. A certain Hebraic humour, of which anticipations had appeared before the Conquest, constitutes one of the main attractions :

þen watȝ a skylly skyualde, quen scaped alle þe wylde ;
Uche fowle to þe flyȝt þat fyþerez myȝt serue,
Uche fysch to þe flod þat fynne couþe nayte,
Uche beste to þe bent þat bytes on erbes ;
Wylde wormeȝ to her won wryþeȝ in þe erþe ;
þe fox and þe folmarde to þe fryth wyndeȝ,
Herttes to hyȝe heþe, hareȝ to gorsteȝ,
And lyouneȝ and lebardeȝ to þe lake ryftes,
Herneȝ and haukeȝ to þe hyȝe rocheȝ ;
þe hole-foted fowle to þe flod hyȝeȝ,
And uche best at a brayde þer hym best lykeȝ.

Finally, the language, an amalgam of English, Scandinavian, and Romance, is handled with power and dignity ; in the later poems, with an austerity which contrasts strongly with the emotional delicacy of *Pearl* and the courtly diction of the speeches in *Sir Gawayne*.

If the identity of the *Pearl* poet is still undiscovered, it cannot be said that much more is known concerning the author of the *Pistill of Susan*. He is styled " Hucheon of the Awle Realle " in the *Orygynale Cronykil* (*c.* 1420) of Wyntoun, who remarks :

> And men of gud discretioun
> Suld excuss and loif Huchoun
> That cunnand was in litterature.
> He maid the Gret Gest of Arthure
> And the Anteris of Gawane,
> The Epistill als of Suete Susane.

Huchoun has been plausibly identified with Sir Hugh of Eglintoun, brother-in-law of Robert Stewart. He was knighted in 1342, travelled to London in connection with the ransom of David II in 1359, and became Justiciar of Scotland in 1360. The term " Awle Realle " appears to refer to the Aula Regis.

On the strength of certain *nota benes* in the Hunterian MS. U. 7.25, Neilson concludes that he has discovered the actual text of Geoffrey, used by Huchoun. Further he claims that Huchoun had read MS. T. 4. 1. in the same library, and, on the basis of this material, wrote a cycle of poems,—the *Wars of Alexander, Destruction of Troy, Titus and Vespasian, Morte Arthure, Parlement of the Three Ages, Winner and Waster, Erkenwald, Awntyrs of Arthure, Pearl, Cleanness,* and *Sir Gawayne*. To assign this heterogenous material to a single author is manifestly an absurdity. In the first place, the dialect of the poems varies considerably ; again, the *nota benes* cannot be said to prove anything ; while such an apparently clear case as the identification of the " Gret Gest " with the *Morte Arthure* is quite uncertain, since Wyntoun states that he was acquainted with no account of Arthur's death. Neither the " Gret Gest " nor the " Anteris of Gawane " has yet been identified, so that we are left with but one poem, the *Pistill*, which can, definitely, be assigned to Huchoun's credit.

The *Pistill of Susan*, extant in five MSS., is based upon the apocryphal story of *Susanna and the elders*. It is written in stanzas of thirteen lines, eight rhymed alternately and followed by a *bob* and *wheel*, cdddc. The story is attractively told, despite some excess of detail, and a passage, towards the close, describes with affecting pathos the interview between the condemned Susanna and her husband :

Heo fel doun flat in þe flore, hir feere whon heo fond,
Carped to him kyndeli, as heo ful wel couþe :
"Iwis I wrapped þe neuere, et my witand,
Neiþer in word ne in werk, in elde ne in ȝouþe."
Heo kevered up on hir kneos, and cussed his hand :
"For I am dampned, I ne dar disparage þi mouþ."
Was neuer more serwful segge bi se nor bi sande,
Ne neuer a soriore siht bi norþ ne bi souþ ;
þo þare,
þei toke the feteres of hire feete,
And euere he cussed þat swete :
"In oþer world schul we mete,"
Seid he no maie.

XX. *PIERS PLOWMAN* AND ITS CONGENERS

During the thirteenth and fourteenth centuries a considerable amount of satirical literature was produced, having as its object the reform of abuses in Church and State. Particularly interesting in view of their anticipations of *Piers Plowman* are the short poems, *On the evil times of Edward II* in the Auchinleck MS. and *Winner and Waster* (c. 1350). In the former, Truth, Simony, Covetousness, and Pride play their parts as allegorical figures, the satire embracing both the corrupt clergy and dishonest officials. In *Winner and Waster* the two disputants plead their cause before the king in much the same way as Peace and Wrong in *Piers Plowman*. The author relates how he fell asleep " bi a bonke of a bourne," and thus introduces the dream-allegory.

The interesting poem, known as the *Parlement of the Three Ages*, may also be included among the anticipations of *Piers Plowman*, if, as has been held, it belongs to the author of *Winner and Waster*. The poet fares out in the month of May to " dreghe his werdes," and, among other things, to shoot at hart and hind. Resting by the side of a stream where blossom the primrose, the peri-winkle, and the penny-royal, he is overtaken by darkness. He perceives a hart and kills it with his cross-bow, after which he falls asleep and dreams. Three men appear before him, representing Youth, Middle and Old Age. Youth is hatless and wears a chaplet of flowers, Middle Age, represented by a man of sixty, is engrossed with rents, manuring, and marling, while Old Age, mumbling and moaning, recites his creed. Youth vows to wear no head-gear till he has performed an exploit worthy of his lady-love. Middle Age counsels him to sell his horse and buy bullocks, whereupon Old Age warns both that the interests of youth and middle age are but transitory, recalling the Nine Worthies, who have, one and all, passed away. Such is the main theme of the poem, the sketch of the Nine Worthies being derived from Jacques de Longuyon. But the author continues with a list of wise men,—Aristotle, Virgil, Solomon, Merlin,—regarded mainly as enchanters and alchemists. The poem con-cludes with a roll of famous lovers,—Amadas and Ydoyne, Samson and Dalida (" death has them both "), Ipomedon and the fair Fere, Generides and Clarionas, Eglamour and Cristabel, Tristrem and Ysoude, Dido, Candace, Penelope, and Guinevere. The *Parlement of the Three Ages* is an attractive piece, and well illustrates the interest of the alliterative school in the technique of the chase, cf. the descriptions of the hart's antlers, the "breaking of the deer," and the attractions of falconry. The most important of English dream-allegories in the fourteenth century was *Piers Plowman*. The type had long been fashionable abroad, particularly in France, where Raoul de Houdenc had written his *Songe d'Enfer* at the beginning of the thirteenth century. But the chief examples of French dream-allegory are to be found in the *Roman de la Rose* of the thirteenth and Deguileville's *Pèlerinage* of the fourteenth century. Between these latter and *Piers Plowman* there are resemblances, which suggest the possibility of direct indebtedness on the part of the English poet.

Piers Plowman consists of a series of visions, more or less loosely welded together. The vision of the "fair field full of folk," with its accompanying pictures of Lady Meed, False, Favel, and Conscience, is succeeded by a second vision, concerned with Piers Plowman and the Seven Deadly Sins. There follow the visions of Do-well, Do-better, and Do-best, an account of a journey to Jerusalem in the company of Abraham, a vision of Christ's entrance into Jerusalem, His crucifixion and death, and a final section, describing the poet's retreat, in his old age, to the House of Unity. In the later sections, the scheme is confused by an endless succession of discussions on social and theological problems. In his old age the poet tended to become garrulous and even pedantic. But the parts are welded together by the central personality of Piers Plowman, at the outset a type of the hard-working, God-fearing labourer, but, in the end, the representative of "human nature united in Christ with the Godhead."

The serious purpose of *Piers Plowman* is at once apparent from the number of references to social and religious abuses. The fierce outbursts against the corrupt clergy, and the insistence on the need for social reform were but signs of the times. The poet makes himself a mouth-piece of the poorer classes, voicing their wrongs

and sufferings. Social questions began to come to the
front about the middle of Edward III's reign. The
frequent recurrence of pestilences had accentuated these
problems, owing to the ravages they caused among the
lower orders. During the plague of 1348, large towns
like Bristol and London were severely affected, and, in
the following year, the whole of East Anglia fell under
the scourge. In consequence, the numbers of the labour-
ing classes were considerably reduced. At the same
time, feudal methods of land-tenure began to give way
before new methods, whereby land was hired out for
fixed sums. Labourers were able to move freely from
place to place, but the *Statute of Labourers* (1351), representing an attempt to fix a definite scale of wages, aroused
much discontent. Socialistic ideas began to germinate,
and John Ball hurled denunciations against the existence
of private property. Meanwhile, religious opinion was
changing rapidly throughout Europe, and a multiplicity
of new orders sprang into being. In England, religious
opinion became more and more anti-Papal, and the
Statute of Provisors (1351), supplemented by *Præmunire*
(1353), was the outcome of popular indignation. But
the most important aspect of the religious movement of
the period is to be seen in the work of Wycliff. He
denounced the begging friars, portrayed in the pages of
Chaucer and Langland, and aimed the fiercest blow at
the authority of Rome. At the moment when the
struggle between Wycliff and the clergy was at its height
John of Gaunt stood out as the most important figure
in the realm. Edward III had fallen into a decline and
died in 1377, the year following the death of the Black
Prince. Richard II, the " kitoun " of *Piers Plowman*,
remained a minor until 1388, and during these years the
struggle between rich and poor, clergy and Lollards,
went on unceasingly.

The author of *Piers Plowman* is an impartial reformer ;
he champions the cause of the masses, but only in so far
as this position is consistent with loyalty to the sovereign.

He chooses to conceal his message under the guise of allegory, yet his purpose is not far to seek. The allegory is, for long stretches, confused and wearisome, and the drift of the argument difficult to follow. But, at his best, the author is an artist of great ability, whose most characteristic note is sincerity. In the early part of the poem, the characters possess genuine human interest. Apart from their names, Lady Meed, Glutton, and Envy are living beings, not merely representatives of typical virtues or vices. In tone, *Piers Plowman* is strongly anti-Papal, and there is much denunciation of pilgrimages, indulgences, and services for the dead. Yet the author's religious position is conservative : he clings to the best elements in the old Faith, and upholds the claims of dogma. The influence of *Piers Plowman* was enormously increased by the fact that it was written in the popular metre, and that the illustrations employed were, in the main, of a non-literary order. The Bible is frequently quoted, generally in Latin, but there is little French matter, though the diction is as composite as Chaucer's.

Of recent years there has been much discussion concerning the authorship of this work. Until 1906, it was generally held that *Piers Plowman* was the work of William Langland or Langley, though his name is not recorded in any contemporary document. This opinion was based on two MS. notes, one in an Ashburnham MS. running " Robert or William Langland made pers ploughman," the second in a Dublin MS.,—" Memorandum quod Stacy de Rokayle, pater Willielmi de Langlond, qui Stacius fuit generosus, et morabatur in Schiptone-under-Whicwode, tenens domini le Spenser in comitatu Oxon., qui predictus Willielmus fecit librum qui vocatur Perys Ploughman." In the sixteenth century, the antiquary, Bale, stated that Langland was a priest and that he was born at Cleobury Mortimer, in Shropshire. In 1870, Pearson attempted to prove that Langley was the true form of the poet's name, on the ground that Langlands are not known in the Midlands of the four-

E.L.C. L

teenth century. Despite the Ashburnham MS. and Bale, the author's Christian name was probably Will, cf.

"I have lyved in londe," quod I; "my name is Long Wille" (B. XV. 148),

and there is no reason for doubting Bale's statement that his birth-place was Cleobury Mortimer.

The MSS. of *Piers Plowman* fall into three great groups, known as the A, B, and C texts, and dated from internal evidence, about 1362, 1377, and 1393–1398 respectively. It is probable that these three texts represent different stages in the progress of the work, due to the author's habit of returning to his task at intervals. In this way, the poem grew under his hands, the 13 *passus* of the A text being extended to 21 in the B text, and to 23 in the C text. But, in 1906 and 1908, Professor Manly put forward a new theory, according to which *Piers Plowman* is to be regarded as of composite authorship. Differences of style and metre distinguish one version of the poem from another, and there are discrepancies between the parts of what has usually been regarded as one and the same text. Much is made of the theory that B failed to notice that certain lines had been lost in the text before him, with the result that the confessions of Sloth and Robert the Robber are allowed to remain in juxtaposition; B cannot, therefore, have been identical with A. But, as Dr. Chambers has pointed out, the provinces of the Seven Sins are wont to overlap in mediæval descriptions, and the theory of the misplaced leaf is not inevitable. Still more convincing is the discovery that as yet the original versions have not been arrived at; a majority of A-MSS. often agree with B, where it has been usual to assume that a difference of reading separated the two texts. Until the originals of all the versions —A, B, and C—have been reconstructed, it is unsafe to speculate on questions of authorship, and the views set forth by Skeat are as satisfactory as any yet advanced.

The poem, generally known as *Pierce the Ploughman's*

Crede, belongs roughly to the same period as the C-text of *Piers Plowman*. Skeat dated it more definitely as 1394, in view of the allusions to Richard II and to Walter Brute, who was arraigned before the Bishop of Hereford in October 1393 on a charge of heresy. The author was apparently a Wycliffite (cf. 1. 528). *Pierce the Ploughman's Crede* owed its inception to its predecessor, but it dispenses with the vision, and the ploughman is conceived less as a type than as an individual. Its starting-point was provided by the opening passage in the *Vita de Dowell* (cf. *Piers Plowman* A. ix. 1–15). The author describes, how, in his search for the Creed, he visited successively the Minorites, the Dominicans, the Augustinians, and the Carmelites, but to no profit. Each abused the rival order and commended its own. In the end, he came upon a ploughman who enlightened him :

His hod was full of holes and his heer oute,
wiþ his knopped schon clouted full þykke ;
his ton toteden out as he þe londe treddede,
his hosen ouerhongen his hokschynes on eueriche a syde,
al beslombred in fen as he þe plow folwede.

Piers the Ploughman's Crede is a powerful satire, providing valuable contemporary evidence as to the degeneracy of the "four orders." The account of the Dominicans with their wealthy foundations is particularly valuable, and concludes with a humorous touch :

þanne turned I aʒen whan I hadde all ytoted,
and found in a freitour a frere on a benche,
a greet cherl and a grym growen as a tonne,
wiþ a face as fat as a full bledder,
blowen bretfull of breþ and as a bagge honged
on boþen his chekes and his chyn wiþ a chol lollede
as greet as a gos eye growen all of grece
þat all wagged his fleche as a quyk myre.

While there has been general unanimity as to the separate authorship of *Pierce the Ploughman's Crede*, Skeat inclined to assign *Richard the Redeless* to Langland. This is a moot point, since imitation is always possible. Phrases like "what is this to mene ?", "in quentise of clothinge," "mete of a myst," "yhote trusse," remind one inevitably of *Piers Plowman*, but the general conception is different, and the date (1399) would place it very late in Langland's career. The political poems provide the true congener to *Richard the Redeless*, its allegory being identical with that of the little piece entitled *On King Richard's Ministers*. The author of *Richard the Redeless* produced his poem during the perturbed period, inaugurated by the landing in England of Henry IV. A partisan of Richard, he gradually lost faith in that monarch and leant towards Henry. He inveighs against De Vere and De la Pole, Richard's favourites, against the royal practice of bestowing liveries and white hart badges, and against prevalent fashions. The king, in his opinion, would have done better to rely upon the nation, as a whole. Henceforth, the stability of the kingdom must rest upon the three orders, since young men of yesterday can no more dispense advice than "a cow can hop in a cage." The incompleteness of the poem has been set down to the disturbed condition of the times, but the prologue seems to indicate that it was actually completed :

> And therffor I ffondyd with all my ffyue wyttis
> to traueile on this tretis to teche men therafter
> to be war of wylffulnesse lest wondris arise.
> And if it happe to ȝoure honde beholde the book onys,
> and redeth on him redely rewis an hundrid,
> and if ȝe sauere sum dell se it fforth ouere,
> ffor reson is no repreff be the rode of Chester !

INDEX

149